# Self-Portrait, with Parents and Footnotes

## In and Out of a Postwar Jewish Childhood

My parents and I, Otwock, outside Warsaw, c. 1954

# Self-Portrait, with Parents and Footnotes

## In and Out of a Postwar Jewish Childhood

Annette Aronowicz

BOSTON
2021

**Library of Congress Cataloging-in-Publication Data**

**Names:** Aronowicz, Annette, 1952- author.

**Title:** Self-portrait, with parents and footnotes : in and out of a postwar Jewish childhood / Annette Aronowicz.

**Description:** Boston : Cherry Orchard Books, 2021. | Includes bibliographical references.

**Identifiers:** LCCN 2021010948 (print) | LCCN 2021010949 (ebook) | ISBN 9781644696200 (hardback) | ISBN 9781644696217 (paperback) | ISBN 9781644696224 (adobe pdf) | ISBN 9781644696231 (epub)

**Subjects:** LCSH: Aronowicz, Annette, 1952- | Jews–United States–Biography. | Jews, Polish–United States–Biography. | Children of communists–Poland–Biography. | Mothers and daughters–Biography.

**Classification:** LCC E184.37.A76 A3 2021 (print) | LCC E184.37.A76 (ebook)| DDC 973/.04924–dc23

LC record available at https://lccn.loc.gov/2021010948
LC ebook record available at https://lccn.loc.gov/2021010949

Copyright © Academic Studies Press, 2021

ISBN 9781644696200 (hardback)
ISBN 9781644696217 (paperback)
ISBN 9781644696224 (adobe pdf)
ISBN 9781644696231 (epub)

Book design by Kryon Publishing Services
Cover design by Ivan Grave. Cover photo from the studio of Andoche Praudel, porcelain ceramics, series on the book, 2021.

Published by Cherry Orchard Books, imprint of Academic Studies Press.
1577 Beacon Street
Brookline, MA 02446, USA
press@ academicstudiespress.com
www .academicstudiespress.com

For Różka

# Contents

# Introduction

## Charles Péguy and Romain Gary—A Quasi-Academic Exploration of Memory

Peter Esterhazy, the Hungarian novelist, ends his huge tome about his aristocratic family with a list of at least one hundred writers from whom he claims to have borrowed sentences.[1] To it he appends a slightly shorter list, documenting specific sentences and their progenitors. For example, Saul Bellow, book 1, sentence 36; Vladimir Nabokov, book 1, sentence 266; Witold Gombrowicz, book 1, sentence 304, book 2, sentence 15.[2] The length of the first list raises the possibility that none of his sentences is truly his own, a position he seems to endorse when he insists that even the word "yes" and the spaces between words are borrowings.[3] This excessive—and humorous—precision also accompanies the second list, since counting to line 266 to find Nabokov's influential sentence, even if it is the same edition as the one Esterhazy was using, is highly unlikely to occur to anyone. Playing with the genre of copyright acknowledgments, Esterhazy is surreptitiously telling us that it is impossible to be original. Every voice is a secret alchemical mixture of many other voices, some traceable, some not. And yet the quirkiness of Esterhazy's own voice as he makes these observations lays bare a paradox. The deeper the impact of the influences, the greater the originality of the voice.

In late November 2018, I suddenly started to write about my childhood and adolescence or, more precisely, about my life with my parents. The direct impulse came from two writers, Charles Péguy, the French poet and philosopher whom I have been reading on and off for forty-five years, and Romain

---

1    Peter Esterhazy, *Celestial Harmonies*, trans. Judith Sollosy (New York: Echo Press, 2000), 844-845.
2    Ibid., 845-846.
3    Ibid., 843.

Gary, the Eastern European French Jewish novelist, whom, up to that point, I had never read. They were born at least forty years apart at opposite ends of the European continent, not to mention everything else that differentiates them. I can recognize their respective influence on a sentence here or there. But it is not a matter of sentences. At stake, is their way of remembering and of talking about memory.

Before entering into my own stories about my parents, I will stay a while with these two authors, thinking about them in the way I am accustomed, that is, as a text interpreter. Nothing shows more the interlacing of one's voice with another. But also, I must admit to having an altogether unhealthy love for ideas, unhealthy if one is a storyteller who must let the story do the work. I have been around good storytellers all my life, not least among which was my mother. I pride myself at not being too bad at it myself, but some dybbuk of an idea inhabits me from time to time that requires another form.

## Péguy

Recently, I read an article about how many steps we need to walk a day to remain healthy, and the debate, based on various empirical studies, is between the canonical ten thousand and the challengers 4,500 and 2,700.[4] I grew up in a world in which people walked and did not count their steps. Now that we do not walk, we have taken to counting them. Much lies buried in that difference.

> To age is to pass. It is to pass from one generation to another, from one time to the next. . . . To age is not to *have switched ages*; it is to *become* of a different age or rather it is to have persevered too long in the *same* age.[5]

These admittedly convoluted words stopped me in my tracks, propelling me to jot down at top speed code words that referred to episodes in my childhood. As my initial jab about walking indicates, I have persevered too long in the same age.

---

4   Gretchen Reynolds, "Even One Extra Walk a Day May Make a Big Difference," *New York Times*, June 5, 2019.

5   Charles Péguy, "Clio: Dialogue de l'histoire et de l'âme païenne," in *Oeuvres en prose complètes III*, ed. Robert Burac (Paris: Éditions Gallimard, 1992), 1174. All translations of Péguy are mine.

Péguy describes persevering too long as gradually becoming of two ages at once, the one in which certain problems were so present that they were simply the air one breathed, and the one in which they disappear from view, replaced by others.

> For years and years . . . you throw everything you've got at a certain problem and you can't solve it and you throw everything you've got at a particular evil and you cannot remedy it. And an entire people throws everything at it. And whole generations throw everything at it. And all of a sudden people turn their back on it. And the whole world changes. The questions asked are no longer the same (there will be enough other ones), the difficulties presenting themselves are no longer the same, the prevailing illnesses are no longer the same. Nothing happened. Everything is different. Nothing happened. Everything is new. Nothing happened. And everything prior no longer exists and everything prior has become foreign.[6]

The primary example Péguy gives of "Nothing happened. Everything is different" is his experience of the transformation of the Dreyfus affair, the event that formed his youth. He relates the visit to his bookstore/office of a young man eager to discuss the affair with him, ten or twelve years later. In the course of the conversation, Péguy realizes that what for him had filled his entire life, affecting his friendships, his choice of careers, his finances, his marriage, and eventually his religion, had become just an abstraction.[7] For the young man to be for or against Dreyfus might still have been of interest, but with none of the costs involved, shorn of the ambient atmosphere. The conversation, even if it referred to Dreyfus, no longer pointed to an event that permeated daily life.

When I said earlier that much is buried in the difference between simply walking and walking as an achievement recorded in number of steps, I meant the whole texture of life. This seems like a very odd comparison to the passionate debates of the Dreyfus affair. Nobody debated walking. But beneath lay an entire understanding of what could and could not be measured, of health and old age, of data gathering, and on what the data was gathered. This is not unrelated to my life's work as a teacher of the humanities. I interpreted texts, a

---

6   Ibid., 1206.

7   One version of this encounter can be found in Péguy, "A nos amis, à nos abonnés," in *Oeuvres en prose complètes II*, ed. Robert Burac (Paris: Éditions Gallimard, 1988), 1308-1312.

most fluid enterprise, even if it required a great deal of training. Internalizing the meaning of those texts, made possible by that training, was a central part in the formation of a human being. I cringe when I pronounce that expression, "the formation of a human being." By the criterion of counting steps, it lacks all precision. Is there even a specifically human being? Walking, or rather what lies beneath walking, has turned into an engagement when it was not one before, an engagement to defend the opacity and fluidity of the human against all algorithmic imperialisms. One wakes up one fine morning to find oneself an underground man.

To remember, then, is to capture the change one has witnessed in the texture of time. But it is not as if the past is an object ready-made for our taking. Neither we nor the past stand still.

> For aging is precisely a process through which one sinks gradually, through which the same being sinks gradually into the same perspectival point in an increasingly distant consideration of the same time period.[8]

We are stuck at one point, our formative years. There is movement nonetheless. As that time recedes, we keep on selecting some events over others, seeing meanings we did not see before, ourselves changing as our perspective deepens. The past is not fixed. Yet, as much as our understandings might shift, we are fixed in a certain period. I would not have focused on the article that reported on measuring steps in the way I did if I were not from another time. But it is the present, with its obsession with measuring everything, that makes me identify a certain activity as my past. Memory is this fluid interplay between a past we shape as it shapes us. Precisely because this operation is so connected to an internal, particular history—unavailable as a standardized narrative— Péguy speaks of memory as what makes for all the depth of a human being.[9] Memory, if it is truly memory, is always that of a particular experience of time. It may echo that of others, but it is never the same.

Péguy's tone about memory and aging in the passages I cited above is profoundly melancholy, without a trace of polemic, although occasionally a faint comical note intrudes. "To age is to have persevered too long in the same age." He seems to put the blame strictly on the aging person, who should not have

---

8   Ibid., 1175.
9   Ibid.

persevered in aging. His tone makes me rue my examples of walking and text interpretation, which make me sound like a particularly unlovable curmudgeon. Memory, it would seem, should be more elegiac, more at peace. Luckily for me, one does not have to go very far to find not only a much more polemical tone in Péguy's reflections about memory, but also a much more polemical understanding of the content of memory as such. Not every act of recall is the genuine article. He distinguishes real memory from what he feels is an altogether different enterprise, history.

As I have already mentioned, memory is always particular, personal. In addition, it focuses on details, without attempting to create an all-encompassing narrative. Some of these details can be corroborated in official documents. Some of them cannot. His example of a memorialist is an older friend of his, Maxime Vuillaume. Taking a walk with him through Paris is to discover what happened at this or that street corner during the time of the Commune—who sat in which cafe, who lived where. It is to see the size of the stones of the sidewalks, the construction sites, and the way they became part of the battle in progress.[10] Engaging details in this way, the memorialist conveys the density of an atmosphere, the very thing missing from official documents. By contrast, what Péguy calls history smooths out the details into a linear narrative, operating like a train running on a track at some distance from the coastline. Unlike memory, it does not follow the contours of the coast, with its twists and turns, and bays openings unto the sea, the ebb and flow, the double life of men and fish.[11] History cleans up all that unruly mess.

To say that the memorialist captures an atmosphere is not quite adequate to what Péguy means, however, for it misses the moral dimension. "Memory is always of war." Memory is always embattled, like a general in a war, or, even more so, like a foot soldier who cannot escape to safety.

> The principal inconvenience of foot soldiers, their principal weakness is that they cannot flee in battle, or rather from the battle, as easily as they would like. . . . The foot soldier alone was irrevocably engaged in the battle's destiny and in the destiny proper to the human being.[12]

---

10  Ibid., 1194-1195.
11  Ibid., 1191.
12  Ibid., 1183-1184.

A life is a series of engagements. We are all foot soldiers, with no way of escaping being engaged. These engagements put us at risk. Regardless of whether we uphold the original commitments or reject them for other ones, we have taken a stand, subjecting ourselves to judgment, to defeat, to loss. In this sense, memory is a kind of confession of faith, an affirmation of what one holds fast to. What Péguy calls history, on the other hand, examines the troops at rest, and reports that a suspender was missing from the uniform of a soldier. It refuses to resurrect the live moral options of the battle as it was fought. It is more comfortable with something that no longer presents any challenge for the present. It walks alongside the cemetery, reporting on what is dead and buried.[13]

Who is the historian, for Péguy? Most of us, surprisingly enough. That is, once we get older, fifty, say, with few exceptions, we tell the stories of our youth through the prism of the vague historical consensus that has built up around the events of that time.[14] We do not go back to engagements or ways of thinking that may deviate from the acceptable story because we do not want to stand out. We want to be on the winning side, as that vague consensus has determined it.[15] The human being will always prefer to measure himself than to see himself, says Péguy.[16] Measurement relies on commonly accepted standards. Seeing oneself, by contrast, does not. The descent into oneself is what human beings fear the most. The word he uses is not "fear" but "terror."[17] Why, one might well ask? It might make us see how flimsy the external support for our life's choices really are. Alternately, we might see those choices and their implications clearly for the first time.

One last part of Péguy's treatment of aging and memory deserves mention, the regret he insists is inseparable from remembering.[18] This is incontrovertible. Aging always involves loss—loss of vigor and the wide-open possibilities of youth, of course—but also a confrontation with what did not get fulfilled, the obstacles one did not surmount, a confrontation with the highly flawed person one turned out to be. But, he adds, "nothing is as great and as beautiful as regret."[19] That is more puzzling. What would make it beautiful and great? Perhaps regret affirms our resistance to being objects of measurement. In

---

13 Ibid., 1177.
14 Ibid., 1192.
15 Ibid., 1189.
16 Ibid., 1191.
17 Ibid., 1190.
18 Ibid., 1175.
19 Ibid.

regretting, we measure ourselves against the commitments buried in the soil of our personal history, manifesting themselves in a myriad of ways. Only the inner eye can catch them, and only the inner eye can detect the distance from the mark.

Péguy often spoke of writing his confessions when he would reach the proper age. He never did reach it, dying at the front at forty-one on the eve of the Battle of the Marne. On the other hand, strewn throughout his later writings are hints of his confessions to be. One example involves a cycle of poems, Victor Hugo's *Les Châtiments*, in which the exiled poet rages against Napoleon III's usurpation and abuses of power. Péguy's commentary, equal parts admiration for Hugo's craft and amusement at some of his artistic and personal quirks, has nothing of the confessional about it, reflecting instead an academic style of literary analysis that he both deploys and mocks. The smatterings of a confession occur later, interrupting the literary analysis.

From counting rhyme schemes, he turns to the atmosphere in which the *Châtiments* were read. Most people did not own their own copy, pooling their money to purchase a joint subscription. Péguy, still a child, read the booklets a teacher lent him, recalling their physical texture, the color of the covers, what illustrations were on which page. Copies passed eagerly from hand to hand, people half concealing them as they walked, since Hugo's work was illegal.[20] The details reflect the poems as more than just ideas, entering not only the mind but also the senses. The description conveys the communal energy, the defiance that a large group of ordinary citizens exhibited against an authoritarian regime. He concludes: "This is what will prevent you your whole life long from giving in to any temporal tyranny, be it liberal or, it goes without saying, clerical."[21] From this early experience derived both his later defense of Dreyfus against the Catholic Church's abuse of power and his even later defense of the Church against the liberal abuse of power. As a man closing in on forty, at the point of rupture between one generation and the next, he sees that the atmosphere in which he grew up has passed completely while it continues to form him still, he who has persisted too long in the same age.

I have taken much from Péguy. I could cite, like Esterhazy, sentences 23 and 24 or 34 and 35 as inspired by his style. But like the organic flow that walking was in the old days, my debt to Péguy cannot be captured in discrete units. Although the passages cited here propelled me to articulate my perseverance

---

20  Ibid., 1097-1099.
21  Ibid., 1099.

too long in the same age, Péguy, three generations before me, was already living in my age, or, at the very least, foresaw some of the consequences of "measuring," of the external "objective" gaze of his time. For some reason, my whole adult intellectual life has been an excited objection to mis-applied measurements. Like a knight of yore, I have ridden, lance in hand, against methods which flatten out what Péguy referred to as the depth of the human being. Since Péguy's time, the turn of the twentieth century, the realm of measurement has expanded beyond measure. I might as well be tilting at windmills. I persist. Although remembering my Eastern European Jewish parents cannot be reduced to just this concern, given the centrality of Nazism and Communism in their history and, consequently, in mine, it should come as no surprise that the horse, its rider, and the lance make their periodic appearance.

I should add that I too remember the texture of the Pléiade edition in which I first read Péguy, and the circumstances in which I received that volume. It was a gift from Pien Pook van Baggen, my teacher's wife, inaugurating a friendship which lasted until she died some forty years later. I was twenty-two that fateful summer of 1974, stuck between two loves and two continents. Unable to move in either direction, I chose graduate school instead. It was by far the best decision I ever made, despite the suspect nature of the timing. Volume three of Péguy's collected prose works, later to be followed by its predecessors, accompanied me into adulthood. It now marks my looking back.

## Romain Gary

Had Péguy lived to write his confessions, I doubt very much that he would have spoken about the painful aspects of his relationship with his mother and grandmother, the two women who raised him, and about his missing father, who died when he was an infant. He mentions all of them, here and there, throughout his work, not in order to relate his personal interactions with them but to evoke their way of life, situating them in a historical context. Within his moral framework, to expose the ugly strands of family relationships was equivalent to a violation of intimacy,[22] and in some pockets remains so even today. Romain Gary, born in 1914, and not in 1873, the year of Péguy's birth, already belongs to a Freudian age, to whose categories he refers at the same time as he resists

---

22 Charles Péguy, "De la situation faite au parti intellectuel dans le monde moderne," in Péguy, *Oeuvres en prose complètes*, 540. "When a son speaks ill of his father and mother, I am wounded in my deepest feelings. I have the impression of an indecency, perhaps the most serious of all . . ." (my translation).

them.[23] *Promise at Dawn*, published in 1960, is very much about the painful part of his childhood with his mother. Yet I would submit that as he reveals it, he also camouflages it. His mother's excesses and derailments appear covered with a strange glory. A woman alone had to raise a child in a world that showed very little mercy. She emerges as the brave, resourceful woman whose love and absolute trust in his future sustained him. In writing her story, Gary proffers to her the mercy that the world has denied her. To do anything else—to foreground the crippling effects of that love—would be to side with the world, to add to the cruelty.

Gary's gesture touched me to the quick, as if I too had this negotiation to make. My mother's excesses and derailments bear a family resemblance to those of Gary. The world was even harsher to her than it had been to Gary's mother. *Promise at Dawn* sent me on my way, which, of course, does not coincide with its author's. For one, Gary wrote a fictionalized memoir, which allowed him to embellish and invent the better to capture the double nature of his life with his mother, the source of his melancholy and aloneness as well as of his verve and humor. Secondly, I am not Gary and my mother was not his mother. As in the case of Esterhazy and his lists of authors, *Promise at Dawn*'s influence is not a matter of individual sentences, although there are some. I cannot help but acknowledge, however, an occasional commonality in content and perhaps style, due, I would maintain, to a common human predicament—the fact of having had parents, and Eastern European Jewish mothers, to boot. Most of all, I recognized in the way Gary combined, transformed, exposed, and covered up the details of his past, the royal road to my own.

An incident he relates early in the book illustrates his approach to his mother's excesses, the simultaneous exposure and camouflage in which he engages. His mother, who had a very hard time making ends meet, would continually crisscross the city of Wilno (modern-day Vilnius), where they were living, peddling hats which she would store in their apartment. The neighbors did not like her, a Russian immigrant in a Polish enclave, and reported her to the police as a possible Russian spy or smuggler. The police come to the apartment, empty out all her boxes, crumple their contents, only to exonerate her

---

23  Romain Gary, *La Promesse de l'aube* (Paris: Éditions Gallimard, 1960), 76-80. The French edition I used differs in some details from the one upon which the English translation is based. I include my own translation, but refer to the equivalent passages in the English version--Romain Gary, *Promise at Dawn*, trans. John Markham Beach (New York: New Directions, 2017), 64-68.

in the end.[24] At first, his mother is crushed by the destruction of her wares and her neighbors' betrayal, sobbing for hours, until, unexpectedly, she springs into action. Dragging the young Gary, no more than eight at the time, she rings all the neighbors' bells on the way down the stairs, summoning them outside into the central courtyard. Holding him tight against her, in front of all the building's inhabitants, she points to him and declaims:

> "Filthy petty bourgeois bedbugs! You don't know with whom you have the honor of speaking! My son will be an Ambassador for France, a Knight of the Legion of Honor, a great dramatic author, an Ibsen, a Gabriele d'Annunzio! He . . ." She searched for something altogether crushing, a supreme and definitive demonstration of worldly success.

> "He will have his clothes tailored in London!"[25]

Gary, decades later, still hears the jeers and mocking laughter that rang out at his mother's words, feeling his face turn red all over again as he writes the scene. He says that no event in his life played a more important role. "I owe to it what I am: for the best as for the worst that laughter became who I am."[26] It is a statement which he chooses not to unpack. Some of what he became we do know, both from the book and from his real biography. "I am today Consul General of France, a Companion of the Liberation, officer of the Legion of Honor, and if I became neither Ibsen nor D'Annunzio, it is not for lack of trying."[27] Most readers at the time would probably have known that he had recently won France's most prestigious literary prize, the Prix Goncourt, thus living up to his mother's expectations. Even his mother's wish about the English tailoring gets fulfilled: "And let there be no mistake. I get my clothes tailored in London. I hate the English cut, but I do not have a choice."[28]

All these marks of worldly success do not prevent Gary from inheriting a great deal of pain from the scene in the courtyard. Years later, he describes his humiliation as an eight-year-old boy in remarkably strong terms, as "one of the most painful moments of my life—and I have known a few." Beyond the shaming in the courtyard, the neighbors physically and verbally harassed him for weeks

---

24  Ibid., 48-50; ibid., 38.
25  Ibid., 50; ibid., 39.
26  Ibid., 51; ibid., 40.
27  Ibid., 50; ibid., 39.
28  Ibid; ibid., 39-40.

on end, pulling down his pants, calling him names.[29] And how could the pain not have come as well from his mother's obliviousness to the independent existence of her son? In her need for revenge, she makes him an object for her use, placing impossible demands on him, as if he alone guaranteed her dignity, as if his only purpose were to embody her wishes. The story Gary tells shows this destructive aspect of his mother's love at the same time as his commentary hides it. In the latter, he focuses on the hate-filled faces of the neighbors,[30] their willingness to ridicule a small boy, and a woman alone. Tongue in cheek, he attributes his slow habituation to ridicule and his ability to rise above it to his mother, making it seem as if it were the overcoming he owes to her, when she is responsible for the shaming in the first place. "I was only eight, it is true, but I already had a very developed sense of ridicule—and my mother did have something to do with it, naturally."[31] The bulk of his commentary, however, highlights her unwillingness to bend to circumstances, her fighting spirit, her ability to hope and trust. "My mother stood straight up under the storm, head held high, holding me tight against her. There was not a trace of embarrassment or humiliation in her. She *knew*."[32]

The pain of being exposed to ridicule will not be put to rest so easily, however, reemerging as his attempt at suicide. Immediately after the torturous scene, suffocating from shame,[33] the eight-year-old Gary escapes to a shed in the courtyard that served as a storage place for wood. Parents forbade children to go inside, given that one unfortunate move could make the logs, piled two stories high, cause a deadly collapse. Gary had been sneaking in anyway, creating a hiding place all his own.[34] This time, in despair, he determines that he will allow the logs to fall on him. He eats his last supper, as it were, a piece of poppy seed cake he found in his pocket, seated in his secret hiding place. As he is about to dislodge the logs around him, a cat suddenly appears, stares at him, comes over and begins to lick his face.

> I had no illusion as to the motives of this sudden affection. I still had crumbs of coffee cake spread over my cheeks and chin, stuck there by my tears. His caresses were strictly self-interested. But I didn't care. The sensation of that rugged and warm tongue on my face made me

---

29  Ibid., 51; ibid., 39.
30  Ibid., 50; ibid., 39.
31  Ibid., 51; ibid., 40.
32  Ibid; ibid.
33  Ibid; ibid.
34  Ibid., 51-52; ibid., 40.

smile with delight—I closed my eyes and let myself go—no more at that moment than later in my life did I wish to find out what there was, exactly, beneath the marks of affection extended to me. What mattered was that there was a friendly snout and a warm and concentrated tongue licking my face up and down with all the appearance of tenderness and compassion. I do not need more to make me happy.[35]

And, then, the even more wry conclusion: "I have always thought since that it is worth having some crumbs of cake on one's person, in life, if one wants to be loved in a truly disinterested manner."[36]

From the nearly deadly consequence of his mother's excessive demands, from the suffocation he experienced, Gary, in his commentary, shifts to a kind of happy outcome, a comical acceptance of the human condition: love is never disinterested. It would be foolish to be too much of a purist in these matters. Better to have something with which to tempt a prospect, accepting the terms in which love presents itself. Of course, it is quite possible to interpret this passage as expressing the author's sense that he could never be loved for himself, hidden beneath the veil of a universal condition. Either way, he displaces the opprobrium from his mother, illuminating, rather, the strange and unpredictable twists emanating from a very painful event. His mother is at once the wounded revenge seeker who pays no attention to him, sacrificing him to her needs, and a courageous, trusting person who sustains him, sacrificing herself for him. Both, in ways that can't be pried apart, made him who he is. This inability to separate what is woven together is the mess of the world, in which it remains good to choose life. After the cat purrs against his nose and bites his ear, he says, "In short, life was worth living."[37]

The courtyard scene illustrates the reason he gives for writing this fictionalized memoir in the first place. His mother, he tells us, had been the favorite toy of the dark forces of the universe—gods to whom he gives names, the gods of a murderous ideologies, of absolutes, of prejudice.[38] He affirms a realm beyond their reach, the sovereign principle of the universe, existing at another level: compassion for human beings, flaws and all. His mother, despite her monstrous demands, is worthy of that compassion because she did exhibit both courage and love. "I wanted to wrest from gods drunk on their power

35  Ibid., 53; ibid., 42.
36  Ibid., 54; ibid., 42.
37  Ibid., 54; ibid., 42.
38  Ibid., 15-17; ibid., 4-7.

the possession of the earth, and give it back to those who inhabit it with their courage and their love."[39] Prejudices and murderous ideologies constitute the surface appearance of the world, unlike compassion, which hides beyond a veil. "I grew up waiting for the day when I could at last extend my hand toward the veil that obscures the universe and discover behind it a face of kindness and pity."[40] It takes trust and hope to discover compassion since it does not seem to be part of the world, or, at least, not a valued part of the world. What can it mean to discover it but to exhibit it oneself?

If *Promise at Dawn* affected me because of Gary's treatment of his mother, it also affected me because of what I recognize as a peculiarly Jewish note. This is difficult to establish in a straightforward manner. Much evidence in the book seems to go against it. After all, Gary's mother went to seek a blessing in a Russian Orthodox Church, and herself makes signs of the cross several times when, as he interprets it, she did not know how else to express her desire to protect him from harm.[41] My mother, admittedly from a later time, could have as little conceived of praying in a church and crossing herself as of traveling to an exoplanet. But beyond his mother's gestures, Gary himself seems to have no sense of Jewish affiliation, even as the victim of antisemitism. He describes a scene in which he is the only one out of three hundred aviators in training who is denied a promotion.[42] The reason, it turns out, is that he was naturalized as a French citizen too recently, code for being not only of foreign origin but also Jewish. With characteristic humor, he remarks, "Another consequence, rather unexpected, of my failure [to be promoted] was that from that moment onward, I felt really French, as if, through this magical smack on the head, I were truly assimilated."[43] The French, whom he had idealized as the embodiment of all that was pure and good, a deeply ingrained view he had inherited from his mother, had exhibited prejudice and small mindedness, becoming ordinary people. He could now be a Frenchman among others, rather than an unworthy foreigner among the noble indigenous population. The exclusionary gesture made him an insider. As comical as this interpretation might be, his commentary on the incident does not distinguish itself by its reflection on the Jewish condition. His distance from it, in fact, can go as far as depicting the witness to a duel he fights, who happened to be Jewish, as a cowardly, venal

---

39  Ibid., 17; ibid., 7.
40  Ibid; ibid.
41  Ibid., 188-191, 239, 249; ibid., 175-178, 221, 229.
42  Ibid., 226, ibid., 208.
43  Ibid., 230; ibid., 213.

and vengeful human being—features an antisemite would cheerfully endorse, as his opponents in the duel, Polish officers, do not hesitate to do.[44] Despite all these counter signs, I insist nonetheless on the Jewish note in *Promise at Dawn*.

The meat of the matter, for me, is the inseparable mix of virile, even military, virtues with a kind of humor that undermines them, or at least does not permit them to reign alone. One thinks of the modern Jewish attempt—both Zionist and socialist—to create the new Jew, physically strong, a soldier, a man of action, a worker, in contrast to the studious weakling of the rabbinic tradition. But a whole other span of the Jewish tradition simultaneously questions the muscular Jewish hero. One thinks of the hapless protagonist in the early films of the comedian Woody Allen, in the American version, but even more so, of his antecedents, the many Yiddish writers, whose heroes, like Tevye in the stories of Sholem Aleichem, show a courage and humanity coinciding with rather than challenging the traditional rabbinic Jew. Gary works in both traditions, and his interweaving of them also involves his mother, of course. The last third of *Promise at Dawn* recounts his time as a pilot in the Free French Air Force during the Second World War. Usually underplaying his own exploits although he was wounded in hazardous missions several times, he unabashedly praises the courage of his comrades, most of whom were killed in combat in order to preserve a France not under the Nazi thumb, or under any thumb. He dwells on their style—their cool-headedness, and good humor in the midst of danger. This is how physical courage manifested itself, as a kind of grace, a freedom of spirit. Accompanying these military virtues is also his prowess with women, which, despite some self-deprecating passages, he is not shy about foregrounding.

But these same virile virtues are shadowed by another set that it would be difficult to reconcile with them. He is a Momma's boy. If he is decorated multiple times as a war hero, it is because his mother made him do it. That is a constant refrain. An amusing, and no doubt completely invented example illustrates this. In 1938, when he comes home to Nice for the summer, having studied in Paris the whole year, his mother orders him to assassinate Hitler for the greater good of France and the world. Nothing will happen to him, she insists. The European powers will negotiate for his release if he is caught. He is quite unhappy about the whole thing. After all, it is summer and he has better things to do than go to Berlin when he could be at the beach. But she does not let go of the idea, and so, under duress, he buys a train ticket, at a discounted rate. At the last moment, his mother changes her mind. He is her only son. They cannot

---

44  Ibid., 321-324; ibid., 290-292.

expect such a sacrifice from her. He reminds her that he has already bought the ticket. The topic switches to how to get reimbursed.[45]

The theme of being forced into heroism because of his submissiveness to his mother appears from the opening chapter of *Promise at Dawn* to the end, punctuating it as a whole. In that first scene, his mother unexpectedly arrives in a taxi, a most inopportune visit, since he is stationed at a military post and is about to be mobilized. She has decided to bring him provisions before he is sent to the front, and to command him in a stentorian voice, in front of all his fellow soldiers, to engage in combat with the greatness of a Guynemer, the French aviator who became a military hero in the First World War. The soldiers laugh at him, but, even if, as he puts it, he does not know if he had ever hated his mother more than at that moment, he is now old enough to give them the finger, and to attempt to reassure her.[46] Later in the book, in an incident in which he is still a boy, she tells him point blank that he needs to come back bloodied on a stretcher rather than to suffer a slight to his honor or hers.[47] One of his very grave disappointments when he comes back from the war a decorated soldier is that he cannot show her all his medals. She had lived for that day, but had died of a diabetes-related illness before war's end.[48] These examples leave out Gary's countless references to plunging again and again into combat because he could do nothing else, given his mother's expectations.

Even his prowess with women is not unrelated to her desire that he be a Casanova, and that the most beautiful women in the world should fall at his feet.[49] When he is not promoted to the rank of officer during his prewar military training as an aviator, as mentioned above, he does not tell his mother the truth, fearing it would be a disappointment she would not be able to bear. Rather, he concocts a story in which he failed to get promoted as a punishment for having seduced the wife of the commanding officer. She is impressed. The only one out of 300 denied promotion, she murmurs. Is she beautiful? Is this a great love?[50] To exhibit virile virtues as a docile act of submission to one's mother infuses them with something quite unmilitary.

I do not take this ironic inflection of the military virtues as a dismissal of them. There is not a single doubt that for Gary they remain great, despite his

---

45  Ibid., 216-218., ibid., 199-202.
46  Ibid., 11-14; ibid., 3-4.
47  Ibid., 145; ibid., 124-125.
48  Ibid., 357-370; ibid., 152-153, 332.
49  Ibid., 29, 30, 233; ibid., 19, 20, 215.
50  Ibid., 232-233; ibid., 214-215.

humor. Rather, his humor indicates that something greater nonetheless exists, and it is not love of one's mother, however strong that impression might be. Strangely enough, it involves a reference to his father, the only one in the book. Gary had had very little contact with him since he abandoned his mother and him when he was still an infant, knowing only that his father and his second family died in the gas chambers in Poland. At one point, he receives a letter which shocks him profoundly. Someone had it on good authority that his father died not in the gas chambers but on the way to them, from sheer terror. "The man who died this way had been a stranger to me but that day, he became my father, forever."[51] Mentioning that his father died of fear would seem, at first, to reinforce the oft-repeated accusation, often made by Jews themselves, that Jews had been cowardly during the war, offering no resistance to their attackers, going like sheep to the slaughter, as the expression went. For those for whom military virtues defined the human, the Jews had allowed themselves to be dehumanized. Gary's description of his father's death seems to do it one better. He wasn't even brave enough to be slaughtered in the ordinary way. Yet, Gary's solidarity with his father, more than his solidarity, his recognition of a filial and thus unbreakable bond at the moment of his humiliating death, turns the accusation on the accuser. One does not reproach the humiliated their humiliation. One stands with them, recognizes oneself in them, giving yet another meaning to the line quoted previously, when reporting his own shaming in the courtyard in Wilno. "I became that laughter." His own humiliation became the source of his empathy and his compassion.

He phrases his coincidence with all who suffer later in *Promise at Dawn* as well.

> My egocentrism is such that I recognize myself instantly in all who suffer and I hurt through all their wounds. This does not stop at human beings but extends to animals, and even to plants. An unbelievable number of people can watch a corrida, look at the wounded and bloodied bull without shuddering. Not me. I *am* the bull. I always hurt a little when the elk, the rabbit or the elephant is hunted. On the other hand, thinking about the killing of chickens leaves me rather indifferent. I can't quite imagine myself in a chicken.[52]

---

51  Ibid., 105; ibid., 90.
52  Ibid., 214; ibid., 197-198.

I hear in this visceral response to the exposed and the vulnerable the echo of an old biblical refrain. The persecution of Jews—Remember that you were slaves in Egypt—becomes a command to protect the window, the orphan, the stranger, an injunction repeated thirty-six times in the Hebrew Bible. Hearing this command becomes the truly human way of being, not in opposition to physical courage—it may, in fact, require a great deal of it—but of another order, nonetheless. I think of the many examples of Jews who could have escaped certain death during the war but who chose to stay with their relatives or with the ones for whom they were responsible.

Everything about this interpretation seems wrong. Where in the passage is there any sense of a command? Gary speaks instead of an inescapable identification or even substitution. Besides, Gary includes animals and plants, going beyond human beings. On top of it, I am suggesting that this sensibility is Jewish. I would like to say several things in my defense. That the visceral reaction to the suffering of others can be interpreted as emanating from a command, one would have to be a reader of the French Jewish philosopher Emmanuel Levinas to explain it.[53] I will leave it alone for now. I would just like to point out, in regard to the compassion that vies with military virtue or, more precisely, accompanies it in *Promise at Dawn*, that Gary is too good a writer, most of the time, to be heavy-handed, a defect not everyone can avoid. Having taken a high moral stance, he deflects it by presenting his sensibility ironically, as a kind of flaw—egocentrism—and escaping through humor, by making an exception for chickens. I choose not to be fooled by these tactics. Few readers would be.

I am also not submitting that Gary would agree that the visceral response to the vulnerable, across all barriers, is a specifically Jewish universalism. A chief characteristic of Jewish universalism throughout much of the twentieth century lay in its refusal to recognize such paltry distinctions as Jewish and not Jewish. When identifying with all the strangers, the windows and the orphans of all the world was one of the dominant ways of being Jewish, it may not have been so important to call it so. But now that this universalism is of another time, it might again be worth recognizing as Jewish the response to the vulnerable—the stranger—outside of any group loyalty, if one wants to keep that sense of the meaning of being Jewish alive. But is it really Jewish? After all, it sounds just as much like a Christian or Buddhist teaching or a version of the

---

53  See, among many other writings, Emmanuel Levinas, "The Temptation of Temptation," in *Nine Talmudic Readings by Emmanuel Levinas*, trans. Annette Aronowicz (Bloomington: Indiana University Press, 2019), 42-72.

French Republican ideal, the latter of which so impressed not only Gary and his mother but also my parents. I agree. But why eliminate the Jewish from this list of possible sources? Each universalism has its own flavor and emphasis. We should honor that.

As should be clear from all of the above, Gary's universalism, his recognition of the human beneath and beyond any other distinctions, is woven through and through with humor. It accompanies his ethical concern, preventing it from being some sort of ideological grandstanding. His great enemy, in fact, the gods he had referred to in the beginning of the book, the ones from which he wants to free his mother, are all misusers of the intellect in one way or another—the ones who fall for anyone in power, making their stupidity sounds lofty and important, the ones who speak in absolutes, which allow them to divide and rule, the ones who make of their prejudices a murderous ideology—Totoche, Merzavka, Filoche, he calls them, indicating in both the French and Russian monikers their international range. There is a nuance of difference between these gods, but in each case, there is intellect devoid of any concern other than the idea, ignoring what the idea might crush or is crushing. Humor deflects ideas, prevents them from being easily turned into weapons. It prevents from turning even compassion into a pious way of dominating others. Gary grew up in highly ideological times—Nazism, Communism. *Promise at Dawn* is an attempt to vanquish the enemy both inside and out, but not with their weapons.[54]

I recognize in Gary's universalism at the very least a version of the one I grew up with. I heard it in my Communist summer camp in songs from the International Brigades, and in songs of the partisans from the Second World War. We young Jews sang about a common suffering and a common resistance, identifying without a second's thought with everyone in the camps and on the battlefield. A common bond with all who were denigrated was the immediate meaning of my parents' history, Jews whose persecution during the Second World War was the very reversal of the human. But, despite his struggle for the brotherhood of all mankind, my father ended up buried in a Jewish cemetery, just as in life he had fought with Jewish comrades in the Naftali Botwin Company in the Spanish Civil War. He performed on the Yiddish stage, although he also knew Esperanto. That Jewish coloring, evident in speech, in gestures, in communal bonds, marked the universalism. Although this too is not the whole story I wish to tell in writing about my life with my parents, it plays a prominent part, nonetheless. I am grateful to Gary for having reminded me of its flavor.

---

54  Ibid., 161; ibid., 136-137.

What follows is neither a meditation on memory in the style of Péguy nor a continuous narrative in the style of Gary. The first section is indeed a narrative of the first sixteen years of my life, the formative period in which I am fixed. The rest, while it includes narrative, is closer to a series of meditations on the engagements and puzzlements that stemmed from that period, in the light of the moment in which I am writing.

# 1

# Myth of Origins

## Warsaw

Of my life in Poland, I remember above all the apartment in which we lived in Warsaw, 5 Opoczyńska Ulica, an address I was proud I recalled forty-eight years later, when I went hunting for the building on my first trip back. It turns out that in the official documents from the Institute of National Memory, we had lived on 7 Opoczyńska Ulica. That 5 was so deeply implanted in me, almost at the level of knowing my own name. How could it show up as a 7, siedem, sounding nothing like a 5, pięć? We had moved once in the course of those six years, which would account for two numbers. But was the 5 the later or the earlier address? These documents of National Memory, stamped with many authoritative seals, have raised imponderable questions.

Five or Seven Opoczyńska Ulica had been a good address. My mother did not talk about it in the glowing way she did about the apartment in Paris, in Montmartre, where my parents lived during the good years right before the war, and some years afterward. Yet when she reminisced about the Warsaw apartment, it was with a hue of pride as well. It was on an upper floor of a modest apartment building in a pleasant neighborhood on a pleasant street, even if unimpressive from the outside. Because Old Mokotów, the neighborhood in question, had been spared the bombing of Warsaw during the war, it became home to a number of Communist functionaries, its old-fashioned apartments, with their nooks and crannies, no doubt preferable to the homogeneous box-like structures built in the Soviet style. The apartment apparently came together with the use of a chauffeured car, upon request. Of this luxury, I have no recollection. For a very long time, a beautiful plaid blanket, of a dark blue background, with black fringes, traveled the world with us, with a stint in New Jersey, Los Angeles, and even Lancaster, PA. It was the throw blanket for winter trips in the official car.

My father and mother in Paris, c. 1949.

I associate our move from 5 to 7 or from 7 to 5 with a big brown spot on the ceiling, the trace of a water leak, and the source of my mother's complaints about humidity. I remember looking at the spot, lying in bed on my back. That memory merges with looking at a big chandelier suspended in the hallway, its crystals glistening in an unusual way, blurry through my tears. I had wet my pants, disappointing my mother's intensive efforts to train me properly, sobbing as only someone who has been betrayed by the order of the universe could sob. But mingled with my sense of cosmic injustice—after all, I had been betrayed by my very own body—were also those crystals hanging from the chandelier and the indistinct way they emanated light. I remember these fused feeling of despair and aesthetic detachment better than any physical object in our environment.

Given the presence of antisemitism in Poland, the thought that we might have had to move, not because of humidity, but because of a hostile concierge has crossed my mind. After all, my father and many others were kicked out of their jobs because the new party leadership had decided that the government had too many Jewish cadres, impeding the Poles' genuine embrace of Communism. But since we moved so close to where we lived before, this explanation seems unlikely. My mother, in any case, did not harbor such suspicions of our superintendent, she, who was to become so prone to suspicions of this kind. She conveyed to me that Jews were different from Poles (those were her distinctions, and everyone else I knew spoke that way at the time, at least in private) mainly through pointing out their food habits. See, she would tell me when we saw the super's wife and daughter, they eat raw onions and that is why they are so healthy. She also attributed our maid's good singing voice to the fact that she drank egg yolks. Maybe because these were other people's customs, she did not attempt to impose them on me, admiring them from afar. In later years, in Brussels, the juice of boiled leeks rose above ethnic distinctions, and I drank tall glasses of it with a repulsion so deep that to this day I cannot prevent a frisson of horror whenever I encounter the vegetable, whether in its solid or liquid state.

My father, mother, and I in Warsaw, c. 1953.

My first six years of life, 1952-1958, the years in Poland, fit within the first decade or so of Communist rule. Given my tender age, it should come as no surprise that I remained completely oblivious of the larger political context in which we found ourselves. I do remember that the word "politics" itself intrigued me. In my mind's eye, I see my father reading a newspaper with the word *Polityka* on the masthead, in bold black letters. I asked him what that word meant. The only problem with this memory is that I could not yet read. It must have been a word I heard among my parents' friends who often congregated in our apartment. The second memory that could in any way be connected to the Communist regime is the expedition we made to the top of the Pałac Kultury soon after it was completed. A gift of Comrade Stalin to the Polish People, the building towered over the city. From the top, for the first time, I saw people not at street level or from the second or third floor windows of our apartment house but from immeasurably high up. They were tiny.

The other great reality of my childhood in Poland was the presence of the Second World War, which had ended a mere seven years before my birth. Had I spent more time outside my apartment, I might have noticed some rubble or some feverish construction, remnants and signs of the destruction of most of Warsaw through German bombing. But all I remember of any outdoor excursion was being sent to buy a head of lettuce in an open-air market around the corner, my mother's strategy for inculcating a spirit of independence, as she tracked my movements from the window above. I did have a tricycle but I managed to ride it straight into a beautiful, tall, polished wooden wardrobe in the bedroom, which produced predictable shrieks of anger. As a result of this sheltered existence, I did not see much of Warsaw.

The war entered nonetheless, through my mother's stories and my father's pinky. In a nook of our apartment, sitting in an armchair, my mother would read me fairy tales, as I perched on a lower stool at her side. Stories of the concentration camps followed the fairy tales, told in the same intimate location of our apartment. Jews, my mother would tell me, were hounded, gathered in camps, and when they thought they were being allowed to take a shower, instead of water, gas would come out and they all died. She would recount this without ever mentioning her own family—the three sisters who had stayed in Poland, her father, two of her brothers. When she did speak about her family, it never coincided with the stories of the concentration camps, and never included what happened to them during the war. They had disappeared, this was much was clear to me, and I knew that at least as concerned those three sisters, it was during the war. She would also tell me of my father's heroism in the camp to which he had been sent. He and a group of comrades shared everything, including the meager tobacco they had, but more to the point, he had cut off the top part of his own pinky, in order not to be forced to do something terrible. I never found out what that something was, and my father never talked about it. I would often play with his hands when we were walking somewhere, tossing the one I was holding high in the air, and then catching it again. That is as far as the communication about the pinky ever went between us.

Given the lack of any Jewish ritual or Jewish learning in our properly Communist household, I, like many others of my generation, inherited my knowledge of being Jewish through my mother's stories about the concentration camps. I use this term because the word "Holocaust" was not in circulation yet, and my mother would not have used the Hebrew and Yiddish word *hurbn*, destruction, to an exclusively Polish-speaking child. To this day I feel uneasy about using the word "Holocaust," as if it carried a meaning not quite matching what I received directly. I did understand, as I listened to my mother's stories, that what happened to the Jews had been particular to the Jews, but I understood this in a diffuse way. It is common today to blame both Jews and non-Jews for not having distinguished, in the twenty years or so after the war, between Jewish destiny—certain death for all—and that of other groups, who suffered greatly but for whom the Nazis did not have total destruction in mind. I feel that I knew this well enough, in an obscure way. Maybe I am wrong, but like the 5 Opocyñska Ulica, it is difficult to let go, precisely because it may capture how many Jews reacted at the time. Jews' lack of emphasis on the singularity of their fate came not only from the fear of drawing attention to themselves after the war but also from a deeply ingrained experience that the disaster had been universal. Of course, in putting it this way, I may be more a product of Communist Poland than I would like to admit. I am grateful, at any rate, that I did not inherit the sense of shame so in vogue at the time about Jews "going like sheep to the slaughter."

One might well ask whether it had been wise on the part of my mother to tell a four-year-old or even a five-or six-year old that people who expected water to come out of shower faucets were delivered gas instead, and that they died of asphyxiation. My mother's notions of childrearing would not pass muster today, and if I were to tally her many real and perceived violations, it would make for a monotonous litany, which, as we will see, I will not be able to avoid altogether. I do not regret at all, however, that she told me this story so early. It has sealed into my otherwise very malleable person the intense reality of good and evil, as a permanent fixed point. Nothing can persuade me to this day that they are mere social constructions or an evolutionary by-product useful for the survival of the species. To erase the absolute nature of good and evil, to relegate good and evil to appearances beneath which hide the real forces that move human beings is an offense to my deepest memory. Deliberately poisoning people has nothing underneath it to explain it. It is rock bottom evil. Figuring out what is good and what is evil in specific circumstances remains a complicated task, but we are not left without images that stand in the background, like commands from Sinai. Perhaps "like" is not necessary here.

My father's shortened pinky may also have been the source of my adoration for him, unabated despite the sixty years since he died. It is not that I remember much about him. Like others of his generation, he had little to do with my education as a small child. In addition, my parents often fought, throwing a wrench into the works. They fought hard. I remember a kitchen knife in my mother's hands once, after a terribly loud scene. Another time, he was banished from the marital bed, and one of them slept in the hallway, in full view of the maid. I was troubled by this public display, both because my father had been banished and because it was public.

My mother had much to be upset about. My father was unfaithful to her. There was also the existential crisis. My father had been a Communist practically since his gymnasium years, from the mid-1920s onward, a volunteer in the International Brigades in Spain, part of the Communist Resistance during the war. Now that he had been dismissed from his post as vice-director of imports in the Ministry of Commerce, with no other means of employment, did he, like many Communists before him, accept this as yet another about-face in the implacable dialectics of materialism? Did he reason as a result that his sacrifice was necessary or, on the contrary, observing the workings of dialectical materialism a bit too close up, did he begin to question the need for sacrificial offerings instead? A photograph of him around this period shows a man grown suddenly old, no longer the elegant rake he had been even five years before, but heavy-set, jowly, with tired eyes.

The economic realities were equally daunting. Where to go? How to make a living once there? France was closed because of the illegal party activities for which my father had been deported in 1949. He would not even consider the United States, even if he had been allowed in. My mother never mentioned Israel, when she recounted their deliberations to me later. Although my father was well educated, he did not have a profession as such, his stint as vice director of imports notwithstanding. He had studied theater in the Berlin of the 1920s, and had acted throughout the thirties and later forties in Paris. In a strange twist, he is given the profession of film actor in one of the dossiers compiled on him by the Polish Secret Service, the UBP. My mother who, in theory, could have helped to alleviate our economic plight had not worked for many years, and although fluent in several languages, was unskilled, with a grade school education. I suspect that the thought that she would have to work again did not even enter their minds. As I write this now, though, I see in a new light my mother's repeated urging that my father, once we were in Brussels, buy the grocery store on the corner. Perhaps this had been her way of offering to participate. Her father has owned a small dry goods store, in which as an adolescent, she had assisted him behind the counter.

To add to the misery, my father, prior to his dismissal from the Ministry of Commerce, had been accused, along with a number of other Jewish Communist officials, of conspiring with the Italian consul to betray the Polish state. It involved Arabian horses. Many years later I discovered that our phone—that beloved black piece of furniture into which I loved to babble with my parents' friends—had become an instrument of state. My name appears in a secretly taped conversation, amidst the exchange of polite questions about family, prior to getting down to business, which turned out to be a dinner invitation. When I saw my name in the official documents, I was disappointed that the secret tapes had not recorded my banter with the man who used to call me *stara kolacja*, old dinner. I still remember the affectionate tone of that friend of the family, teasing me in response to the way I was using vocabulary that I had not quite mastered. Stara kolacja didn't make it into history, a casualty of the technological limitations of an earlier time.

My father's unfaithfulness, coupled with my mother's suspicions that he was unfaithful, about which she was sometimes right and sometimes wrong, put me in the unhappy situation of being my mother's weapon. I was hers and was to show my loyalty only to her. It is the one matter for which I cannot forgive her, perhaps because I cannot forgive myself. Other children may not have been as dutiful in obeying her edicts. When she told me to stop speaking to my father for a determined length of time, days on end, I complied, not addressing or answering him. When she complained about my father's spending, I echoed these complaints. "Why did you buy everyone drinks when we have no money," I reproached him one of the times he took me with him to play billiards with his friends. The result not only of these paltry events but also of my mother's always present line in the sand is that every longing of love turns into a betrayal.

My father and I in Otwock, c. 1954.

It is not an uncommon bind. Some people try to undo it later in life. The hairdresser tells me that she kept the father of her daughter away, not allowing him contact because of his irresponsible ways, taking on the burden of parenthood on herself alone. Her daughter, now an adult, in trying to free herself from exclusive allegiance to one parent, has reversed her loyalties instead. Not only does she have a close relation with her father but also refuses to come to her mother's assistance. Lately, the hairdresser sighed, her daughter would not come to help her get into the bathtub, although she had been injured and could not do it on her own. Not quite freeing, I say, but it could get worse. An accomplished French Jewish philosopher describes in her memoir how as a small child during the war, she came to prefer an elegant and worldly Gentile woman to her emotionally overwrought, erratic mother, choosing to stay with the Frenchwoman when the war ended, repeatedly returning even when her mother brought her back forcefully. When the burden of her behavior during the war years became too much for her as an older teenager, she stopped visiting the Frenchwoman, just as the latter was going blind.[1] A year after her memoir came out, at the age of sixty, the French philosopher killed herself. One

---

1    Sarah Kofman, *Rue Ordener, Rue Labat,* trans. Ann Smock (Lincoln: University of Nebraska Press, 1996).

does not presume to know the causes of a suicide. The memoir, though, was so filled with pain over a series of betrayals she could not reverse that I could barely read it. As for me, I have found no key to unlock that meek obedience of a long time ago, thus belonging to the large category of those who neither freed themselves nor committed suicide.

The documents from the Institute of National Memory show that my parents applied to leave the country many times, from 1956 onward, to visit relatives, they say. Eventually, in 1958, we were given the proper papers and allowed out. My father went first, to Brussels, where they had decided to try their luck, in order to prepare our way. My mother and I followed six months later. I remained, of course, completely unaware that our trip was not a solitary one. Approximately fifty thousand Jews, a large proportion of the remaining Jewish population of Poland left it between 1956-1959, in response to the anti-Jewish climate. Of this exodus, I retain only two very personal details.

We left Poland by train but somewhere in the course of our journey, we found ourselves on the wrong platform, and risked missing our connection. Time being of the essence, my mother did a daring thing. She lowered herself down to the tracks, crossed over, and climbed up on the right platform on the other side. Not only was I afraid that she would be in some passing train's way but also that she would not be able to pull it off, given her tight skirt and heels. The tight skirt was not the tight skirt of my generation. This was 1950s Poland. Nonetheless, it had not been designed to ascend and descend anything but stairs. In my memory, I was worried about her but also embarrassed. This was not a decorous way of behaving, I knew, and I was a decorous child. I have always remained decorous, aware of spoken and unspoken rules and extremely loathe to break them. My mother had only impatience for my conformism. Tellingly, I do not remember what I myself did at the moment she descended the tracks. I must have followed her.

Once on the train, a similar thing happened, only in reverse. There were no extra seats in our compartment, and I gallantly stood up and gave my seat to a Polish priest. Since our train journey was to be three days long, my mother was no doubt right that the standards of etiquette did not apply. Without reprimanding me directly, she made very clear that the nobility of my gesture was completely lost on her. I continued to stand solemnly in the middle of the compartment. I was not allowed, however, to leave Poland in this sacrificial pose. Once we were at some distance from Warsaw, I remember stretching out on the train seat, and sleeping soundly, but not so soundly that

I did not overhear the praise of my good intentions that my mother and the priest exchanged.

This journey from Poland to Belgium was my first migration but the third major one for my mother, following her earlier one from her home city Kalisz, in Central Poland, to Paris, in 1933, and from Paris to Warsaw in 1950. She was to experience two more, the ones that permanently took us out of Europe, the first to New Jersey from Belgium in 1962, and the second from New Jersey to California in 1968. But we were still in 1958, and this being my first journey, I took it in stride, too little to yearn for anything left behind. I did not know then that I would soon lose the Polish language, and even when I did, I didn't register it as a loss. Only now, a lifetime later, when I try to speak it, with abrupt halts in the middle of sentences that I cannot complete, do I feel the presence of a lost world. It is a strange joy, as if buried in each of those sounds lie carefully compressed all seven volumes of Proust's *Remembrance of Things Past.*

## Brussels

As eventful as those four years were, Brussels itself does not belong to our family's larger history the way Poland and France did. It was a place of transition. Within those years, my father died and my mother showed the first signs of an illness that became flagrant fifteen years later. I was eight when my father died, and it is an event I missed completely while being in the same room. My mother had sent for a doctor in the middle of the night. Convalescing from a heart attack, my father had suddenly taken a turn for the worse. When the doctor arrived, he noticed that he lacked a needed medication. Even though at that hour the pharmacies would be closed, I ran down the neighboring streets searching for one, absorbed in my sense of drama, and knowing obscurely that this was the wrong emotion. The false note, if one can call it that, continued when I came back empty-handed. I reproached the doctor for not having brought the right medicine, all the while looking at my reflection of the bedroom mirror. My father was emitting sounds that I still hear, with my mother bent over him. At some point those sounds must have stopped but rather than a sudden quiet, I hear my mother's hysterical crying. I too start crying, but not in response to my father. I was responding to my mother.

He must have died close to morning because soon thereafter a crowd of people appeared in the house. I was dispatched to friends of my mother, the Urbachs, whose daughter Eva, around my age, my mother had designated as a model of discipline and resoluteness in comparison to my flabby ways. Madame Urbach had strict policies about the mixing of liquids and solids at mealtimes. One was to drink only an hour after a meal. I spent a couple of days there, obeying the local customs. The house seemed very modern to me, geometric, with a garage. In the meantime, the first of my father's two burials occurred, in a nondenominational cemetery somewhere in Brussels.

When I came home, my mother did not speak about my father at all, other than to tell me that my father had been taken to a hospital and that he would return when he was better. One day, months afterward, when looking out of the window I noticed a man wearing a raincoat similar to my father's, I called my mother over and broke the silence. She rebuked me sharply. It was well over a year after his death that she acknowledged that he had died, in early fall. I remember the softness of the few leaves on the ground, and the already more subdued sunlight. It was a very quiet slipping into the reality of our situation. I knew from the beginning, of course, that my father had died. When the school year started, and we were supposed to fill out our parents' names on an official sheet of some description, without too much hesitation I put "deceased" next to the blank where my father's name would have gone.

So many years later, the chronology of events around my father's death wobbles. When did my mother express alarm that she had ridden to the end of the tramway line and back as if she had lost consciousness? Was that before or after that walk on the leaves in the fall? Was it before or after that she told me, one late afternoon, as she was picking me up from school that she was feeling low. "J'ai le cafard," she said. It was the first time I had heard the idiom. It faintly amused me, maybe because cafard also means cockroach but I am not sure I knew that then. We shared the pleasure of the expression, somewhat displacing its content. If those two instances could fit on either side of the walk on the leaves, her accusation that I was responsible for my father's death could only come afterward. I was incensed. His death, I knew, had nothing to do with the many dolls he had brought me from his business travels, the purchase of which my mother claimed made him work too hard. I knew that I had wronged him terribly. But he hadn't died because of those stupid dolls, so fancy, that my mother aligned in rows in a corner of my room, as if creating an altar. Even as images of what I had done gripped my heart, I also knew that I was a child, something that my mother did not seem to realize in equal measure. How could she not know something so basic that even I knew it? My mother's reaction protected me in a strange way. I directed my anger at her, leaving only a portion for myself.

Looking back, I would say that this complex of events, among its many consequences, instilled in me a sense for the inner life. One's experience could be completely ignored or misunderstood, remaining invisible and inaudible despite one's best efforts to make it as plain as daylight. The attempt to communicate that experience, the difficulties facing that transmission, its success in rare but key instances, have always stood at the center of my world. It may even explain why, as a university student, I chose to study religion, despite the contempt I had inherited from the ambient culture about those benighted people who practiced it. I learned to see religious expression precisely as the defense of an experience whose confirmation from the outside was not assured, and which always ran the risk of obliteration. Since in more recent times we seem hellbent on equating or replacing human interiority with sophisticated algorithms that bypass our self-understanding, I feel a certain elation. I am in my element. I must admit, though, that my mother's version of reality was slightly less threatening than an algorithm. It did not come clothed with objectivity.

Coming back to May 1960, the time of my father's death, I did not yet have this providential understanding of my destiny. When the school year ended, my mother sent me to a sleep away summer camp for two months. At age eight, with the exception of those days with the Urbachs, I had never been away from home. Summer camp became a regular part of my life for the next eight years, three summers in Belgium, and five summers in the New Jersey/New York area. During the Belgian years, it accounted for the only continuous stretch of popular culture that I ever managed to appropriate, mostly Soviet war songs that we learned both in the socialist Zionist camp I was sent to in July, and the Communist camp I was sent to in August. It was in one of those camps, at age nine or ten, that I experienced my first crush, and my first awareness of my face as the face of a girl who might or might not be pretty. (I concluded to my great surprise that I was.) That first summer, however, was a summer of shame. I wet my pants yet again, and everyone saw. I remember being taken to a separate area, probably the camp's infirmary, wailing so uncontrollably that something like the experience of the chandelier repeated itself. The sounds were emanating from me, but it was as if I were listening to them not from the bed inside but from the courtyard outside. I had split in two.

I do not understand why this story is so difficult to tell, even today. Surely decades ago, I must have realized that I was only eight, that it was my first time away from home, that the other children were not angels, and that my world was anything but stable. But nothing can erase the shame. Not too long ago, a friend who became enamored of cognitive behavioral therapy told me about techniques he learned to avoid fear of humiliation or dwelling on it if it did happen. What is the worst-case scenario, we are supposed to ask ourselves? After all, what really happened? At most, we experience momentary distress, and then everyone forgets about it. Let us not make mountains out of mole-hills. If they work for someone else, who am I to deny such useful techniques? All I know is that that humiliation the first month of camp became so deeply lodged that it could not and cannot be reached, not by keeping silent and not by speaking, and not through the recitation of formula. It had many effects, some rather unexpected. I soon became very "popular," not that year but the following year or two, a perfect little camper. Once we moved to the States, and I was sent to the Golden Chain Camp in New Jersey, I even won an award, "best in bunk," for which I was given a small, gold-plated medal of the Virgin Mary. I was no longer going to exclusively Jewish camps, but my mother's ecu-menicism stopped at the Virgin Mary. Her displeasure went beyond the medal to the award itself. She did not think behaving in such a way as to win the "best in bunk" award was a good sign for my future.

The other humiliation that summer I have talked about even less. On the surface, it was not mine but my mother's. In the last two weeks of camp my mother appeared as a camp counselor of sorts, for another group of children. She was considerably older than the rest of the staff. Most likely, some mem-bers of the Jewish organizations in Brussels that had funded my camp stays to help my mother thought it might be of further assistance to her emotion-ally and financially to employ her in this fashion. Alternately, this might have been the price she had to pay to have me go to camp for free. At any rate, once she got there, everyone made fun of her. One fuzzy detail comes back to me, her sweeping the floor in one of the sleeping areas. On that occasion someone said something about her behind her back, not only within earshot, but as if addressed to me. I screwed up all my courage and defended her. My code of honor might have come from the children's version of *The Three Musketeers*. I was a precocious reader. As I recall, I was already playing d'Artagnan in our children's games in the school courtyard, even if the other children remained in the dark about my character. My mother did not know I had defended her, and she probably did not notice the comment behind her back. I should be proud of that moment, but I am not. I was profoundly ashamed of her. It was much easier to swing my imaginary rapier at the king's enemies than it was to admit I was her daughter.

As to my mother's incipient illness, its strongest manifestation during this period was our constant moving from one apartment to another. The first move was reasonable. The apartment on 10, rue Dodonnée in Uccles, had been too expensive for us, given my father's unsuccessful struggle to establish an import/export business. The debts he left when he died made a less costly apartment even more of a necessity. We would not have been able to afford anything at all, if it had not been for the financial help of my parents' friends, who would appear periodically from Paris. That is how I got to know Boris, my father's friend from childhood, and Pola, my mother's friend from the war period, becoming very close to each of them in later years. My mother's sister Hela, and her husband, Jacques, who lived in the United States, probably provided the bulk of the help. Upon my father's death, my mother started working in the needle trade, as she had done as a young woman, but she could not find full employment. Not being a Belgian citizen presented an obstacle. At least part of my mother's decision to emigrate to the United States was to stabilize our civil and economic situation. There she could support us, she was sure. In the meantime, we moved three other times in a two-year period, each move precipitated by her certainty that the neighbors, downstairs, upstairs or across the street, had something against her.

I remember strictly nothing about those apartments, except for a mantelpiece with a framed photograph of my father on it, and a metal tub that my mother would periodically take out of some closet and fill with hot water for a weekly bath. In one of those apartments, though, an event arises out of many others. In anticipation of my mother's birthday, I had hinted to her in the previous days that I had a present for her. It was the first time I was offering her a gift, a small notebook that I had unearthed somewhere, whose color and shape pleased me. I do not remember her words, just her uncontrollable anger that that this was all I had chosen to give her. That night, after a day in which she refused to speak to me, lying next to her, I listened for her breathing and could not hear it. Frantic, I kneeled by her side of the bed, and pleaded without being able to stop. Please forgive me, please, again and again. I remember my terror but also, even more, hers. When I got back to bed, I prayed silently that my mother would live until I was twenty-two.

A year or so afterward, we managed to gain permission to emigrate, after a two-year waiting period, and in 1962, we sailed to New York. In New Jersey, where we settled, there was no mention of hostile neighbors, although some of my mother's convictions about the ill intentions of others switched to her bosses and co-workers. The neighbors were to reappear again some years after we moved to Los Angeles, and, in my mother's mind, their dislike of her turned into very complex persecution involving her every move, down to her every breath. But that is a story for another time. While we lived in Brussels, her episodes were intermittent. She still had some good friends, also widows, whom she entrusted with the care of my father's grave when we left, having moved him to the cemetery in which their husbands were buried, a Jewish one this time, in part to facilitate this task. During those two years after my father's death, she and I would go for short vacations to Knokke le Zoute on the North Sea, occasionally splurge on a movie or restaurant, and eat Belgian fries from the triangular paper cones that were sold in kiosks on street corners.

My mother, on the right, with her two widowed friends, Madame Pinczewski, center, and Madame Frieda, on the Belgian seashore, c. 1961.

I returned to Belgium only twice since 1962. The first time was a mere ten years later, while I was studying abroad in France. My mother had suggested I go see how our belongings were doing in the basement of her friend, Madame Pinczewski. We had left behind when we boarded the Queen Elizabeth II some remnants of the splendors of Paris and Warsaw, too expensive to transport. We would send for these items when our circumstances improved. In the ten years since our departure, they had never improved enough, but I suspect that my mother was just as happy to have the past stay exactly where it was. She was nonetheless curious, and thus her request that I look into it. In Madame Pinczewski's basement, a large area was covered with white sheets. Lifting them, I glimpsed sculptures, and paintings, and many, many books. From all of this, I retrieved a tiny pewter vase and a set of small Polish figures, a male and female dancer, dressed in regional costumes. The young woman had ribbons of many colors attached to her tresses, and both she and her partner wore elaborately embroidered vests over white blouses. My mother could not believe that these had been my choices, these baubles, when there were so many valuable objects. It wasn't my fault, I thought. She should have given me instructions. But beyond that I was following the moral of a couple of stories she would tell frequently. One was set in Tel Aviv, in a cafe called Miao-Miao. Polish Jews would sip tea, embroidering tales of the enormous wealth that they had left behind, in case anyone confused their current humble circumstances with their real stature. Not the least point of the story was linguistic. Miao Miao is a homonym of the Polish *Miał, Miał*, "He had, he had." We would laugh. The other story was a ritual recitation of sorts, told many times. My mother had been arrested in Paris, in the summer of 1942, during the great round up known as *La Rafle du Vel d'hiv*. Most of the thirteen thousand Jews—mostly old men, women and children—forced into that sports stadium, eventually perished in Auschwitz. When the French police came to her door, my mother would tell me that unlike other Jews, she did not take pots and pans, and many suitcases. She merely threw a coat over her shoulder. When she decided to escape from the stadium, she could simply walk out, since she was not burdened with belongings. Although not attributing her escape merely to this, she always made a point of inserting this detail in the ritual retelling. With such stories in my background, how was I supposed to know she wanted me to retrieve valuable objects?

Several years after my visit, Madame Pinczewski's basement flooded. My mother did not mourn much. The higher social status that those objects represented were a fond memory, with which she warmed herself occasionally. But although she complained of arthritis and exhaustion, being a factory worker was a source of pride for her. She was supporting us through the work of her hands, finally independent. This in no way contradicted her yearning for an easier life, but she had come from humble economic origins, and was not ashamed of them. When I think of those white sheets now, I experience a strange greed I did not have when I was twenty. I thirst to lift them again, to see which books were in that library, in which languages. But beyond this glimpse into my parents' cultural world, I must admit to craving outright ownership, not only of the books, but also of the art work and the beautiful household items. I want, against the insecurities of old age, an inheritance, as if I had grown up in a stable family in a century not torn by war and private sorrow. Luckily for me, that desire cannot be realized. In the meantime, although the Polish dolls disintegrated, ribbon by ribbon and shred by shred, the pewter vase, too small for even one small flower, remains a marvel of grace, more than a half century later.

Because that first visit back to Brussels took place only ten years after our departure, I still knew some people, experiencing the intensity I have to come to know since in other places—the brief rekindling of bonds with people with whom one once shared a life. My mother would often say that she had been lucky with her friends, and Madame Pinczewski was such a friend. Very happy to see me, she cooked a dinner to which she also invited Madame Frieda, and when I was ready to leave, insisted on going down with me to make sure I took the right tramway, standing short and square beside me, pressing some money in my hands for the fare, even though I assured her I did not need it. Something similar happened when I met with the Kazarians, the parents of an elementary school friend of mine, Aida. After my father died, they bought our Louis XV-style furniture, which I suspect today was also a way of helping us out. Aida was unrecognizable. From the little girl I had played doctor with, she had turned into a great beauty, and, at twenty, had recently married. She and her husband looked like young divinities. After a more private meeting in a cafe, Monsieur Kazarian invited me to join them at a big family celebration in an expensive restaurant, and insisted that I take one thousand francs, a very generous sum of money. With Madame Urbach, the bond took a different turn. She took me into her confidence, no doubt mistaking my ability to navigate my way around cities and countries for maturity. My father had drunk himself to death, she said. He didn't die of a heart attack but of a broken heart. I do not remember what she attributed the broken heart to, perhaps also a sign of her friendship.

The second time I returned to Belgium, it was to attend a conference in Leeuwen. Thirty-six years had passed since my visit at age twenty, and I no longer knew anyone. Since my father was buried in Brussels, it occurred to me to visit his grave. As I write this I found it odd that the thought had never crossed my mind before, not in 1972 when I went to look inside Madame Pinczewski's basement, and not during the many subsequent trips to France, with Brussels only a short train ride away. Maybe it is the desire to visit his grave forty-eight years after his death that needs explaining. The product of an imperceptible chain of events, once the desire arose, it was tenacious. It turned out that some tenacity was indeed required. Among the items buried in the ash heap of history was the cemetery's name. No one who could possibly have known was still alive. Letters I sent to the local Belgian authorities had produced no results. Once at the conference in Leeuwen, I insisted on collaring various

Belgian scholars whom I had just met, briefly explaining what I was looking for. Someone local knew someone else local. The problem was solved in an hour. Armed with the name and address I needed, I took a train to Brussels and then a taxi. It was a long ride, to the outskirts of the city. The cemetery was deserted, except for one solitary visitor. Watching his movements out of the corner of my eye, the plot and row number in hand, I proceeded to look for my father's grave. Finding it was a moment of explosive joy.

I had intended to bring flowers, as I always do when I visit my mother's grave in Los Angeles. But the area was as deserted outside as it was inside, with no stores in sight. I noticed a stone vase had been built into the horizontal concrete slab, which also was the case for many of the neighboring graves. Perhaps Madame Pinczewski and Madame Frieda, when tending their husbands' graves, had also put flowers in my father's vase. They all stood empty now, and the explanation was not merely the inevitable passage of time. Taking a walk around, I noticed an engraved warning in a newer upper section of the cemetery. In several languages—French, Hebrew, and Yiddish—it warned mourners not to bring flowers, as it is not in accordance with Jewish custom. A large receptacle with pebbles had been positioned at the entrance, indicating the proper Jewish commemoration. I took a few of the small stones and placed them on my father's grave. I appreciate the custom of the pebbles very much. They leave humble traces that flowers cannot. Yet, despite my desire to recover all the lost meanings, that sign annoyed me. In the cemetery in Boston where my friend Geoffrey Froner was recently buried, a similar stern warning was also affixed against a wall, including besides the flowers, all sorts of other forbidden objects. The bereaved blithely ignored them, expressing their bond with the dead in the way they knew. In this respect, I belong to the generation of my parents more than to the generation of those who came after and put up the sign. Surely, a little beauty, even if it is expressed in the same way as that of the Catholic cemetery on the other side of the wall, cannot take away from all those Hebrew and Yiddish names and patronymics, that profoundly Jewish history buried beneath the stone slabs.

My father's gravestone spoke of his history in the intensely abbreviated way that the genre requires. The inscriptions were in Hebrew and French, the Hebrew revealing his name as Yaakov, son of Moshe, and the French revealing him to be Yasha, the diminutive of his Russian name. He was Jewish, he was Russian-speaking. He had been born in Wilno in 1905, and had died in Brussels in 1960. As the French also indicated, he had had a wife and daughter. My mother had had engraved at the very bottom, "à mon cher époux, à mon papa bien aimé, nos regrets." Clearly, he also spoke French. Perhaps today one would feel more liberty to have put something more personal than "to my dear spouse, and to my beloved father, "especially since I never called my father papa. It had been *tata* or *tatiush*, even when we switched to French at home. But there was a way of doing these things at the time, and my mother wanted to do them right. Among the things she wanted to get right was the size of the headstone. It was the tallest in the row.

Perhaps more indicative of my father's history than anything on the headstone was the fact that his grave was indeed in this cemetery, rather than in the cemetery in which he had originally been placed. It is a story I have told often. My mother had originally decided to have him buried in a nondenominational cemetery, which just means a non-Jewish section of a public cemetery. As she explained it to me much later, my father's friends, all Jews, had argued that it would not do for a lifelong Communist who had worked for the erasure of all differences between peoples to be buried exclusively among Jews. She had acquiesced. The reason she had always given me for the transfer was that since we were leaving Belgium, she wanted Madame Pinczewski and Madame Frieda to have easy access to his grave, and so moved him to where their husbands were buried. The documents I now have about the two cemeteries reveal that she had him moved much earlier than our departure date, a year and a half earlier. We may not even have known that we would get permission to emigrate at that point. I think my mother moved my father to a Jewish cemetery because we were Jewish. My father's universalism was Jewish. I came to appreciate this choice of hers. I have to admit, though, that that afternoon, walking among the graves, and reading headstones, I became curious to see what that other cemetery was like. I know that one cannot dance at two weddings with one rear end, as the Yiddish expression goes. But my father did dance at two weddings, in defiance of the physical limitations. Maybe the other cemetery indicated just as well or better the two weddings he had danced at.

## Weehawken, New Jersey

My mother and I lived in Weehawken, New Jersey, from November 1962 through the end of June 1968. The dates of our crossing the Atlantic Ocean on the Queen Elizabeth II—November 16-21—coincided with the Cuban missile crisis. Life on earth could have come to a fiery end, but for me, the entire universe during that five-day voyage narrowed down to sea sickness. No news had reached me of the larger danger facing the planet. I lived the fabled sixties in a similar political fog. It wasn't as if I did not notice the civil rights movement, the Vietnam War, the changes in sexual mores and in dress codes. I noticed but as if from a great distance. I was only sixteen when we left for Los Angeles. But the distance had at least something to do with the language maps typical of immigrants.

In Brussels, after a year of struggling to learn French, I switched to it at home as well. My mother had not insisted that I continue to speak Polish, although she often addressed me in it. Because both she and my father spoke French fluently, I do not remember feeling that the world of the home and the world outside were sealed off from each other, maybe because so much of my world remained the world of the home. Once in the States, the situation was different. My mother tried to learn English, enrolling in night classes at the local high school, but she was too tired to absorb much after a full day of work, and eventually quit. She bought a television about two years into our stay, a long rectangular piece of furniture, with four short legs. Its cost, a hundred dollars, made me marvel at my mother's extravagance. We watched it for two hours almost every night—all the shows of the period: *My Three Sons, Father Knows Best, The Donna Reed Show.* My mother's English did not improve much. Relatives urged me to speak English at home. I had learned it so quickly, and how else would she learn? But French remained the language of home. In a way, it was not a decision since one cannot turn one's intimate communications into language drills. In another way, it was very deliberate. I did not want to speak English at home. Speaking French was a way of remembering.

This meant that the outside world and the inside world did not coincide. I have always liked the lag between them, and, insofar as it was up to me, have perpetuated it. It has made me alternately a puzzle and a source of frustration to others, and occasionally even to myself. I am impervious to arguments about the most efficient way to do things, ignorant of what the first person on the street knows about popular music or movies. My third-generation American cousins, by contrast, expend energy to coincide with the correct date of the calendar and to live plum in the middle of New Jersey. To willfully lag behind or be elsewhere while here is illogical. They are right, of course. It is too late, though, and insofar as I have a commitment, it is this desire for distance, which always runs the risk of being mere silliness. In the 1960s, I had nothing to do with it. The distance produced itself. Since then, although I have become aware of the political and social life around me, a peculiar distance tags along nonetheless. I read the paper every day, very attentively, just to maintain it.

All this theorizing misses the most obvious reason for the fog in which I lived the sixties. Like others my age, I focused on carving out a world apart from the one I had with my mother. In no way a simple matter, it left little room for anything else. My struggle was eased somewhat by our proximity to my cousins. We lived two apartment buildings down, on the same block, 51st Street, the border line between Weehawken, West New York, and Union City. The father of the family, Max, was my first cousin. Because my mother had been nearly twenty years younger than her sister Hela, who happened to be Max's mother, it made me the age of Max's children. It was with them, at least the older two, that I played all sorts of games in the many courtyards attached to the aging apartment buildings. Since my mother rarely came home from work before six, I would also spend much time in their apartment after school, watching *Bugs Bunny* and *Rocky and Bullwinkle*, or talking to Florence, Max's wife. She would set a tall glass of milk before me, and I would eat the pink-topped snow cones and yellow twinkies of the era. The cold milk was at least as exotic as the twinkies. I do not remember what I drank before then, but it wasn't plain milk. She would also help me out with English expressions in the beginning. Ricky Totorro had come over to me and called me sweet, I told her. What did that mean? It was a compliment. She also consoled me about the glasses I broke while playing running bases with the boys. Now I could get rid of those unfashionable wire rim ones I had brought over from Europe. I rather liked those glasses, but her positive take on the fact that I had run straight into a wall thrilled me. I had not encountered this before. This is not to say that my cousins lived in a calm environment. Max was almost as lacking in psychology as my mother, and there were memorable scenes between him and his sons. But for me, the fifth-floor apartment at 17, 51st Street was a sanctuary.

One source of my difficulties in those early teen-age years was my mother's insistence that I accompany her everywhere. Once, for instance, she took me to a New Year's eve ball in New York City, at the *Arbeiter Ring*, the Workmen's Circle. By the middle of the 1960s, this organization was socialist only in memory but it retained the Eastern European Yiddish-speaking atmosphere that my mother must have known all her life, even in the more assimilated Jewish Communist circles she frequented through my father. At that ball, a courtly gentleman, one of our neighbors on 51st Street, who lived with his wife in an adjacent building, asked my mother to dance. He held her by her lower back, almost by her rear, and we laughed about it afterward. He was very tall and must have gotten confused, we said. But despite the fact that observing this milieu, I already knew, could only improve my storytelling skills,

I also had the indistinct feeling that at fifteen I should not be attending New Year's eve balls at *Arbeiter Ring* with my mother. The desire became more distinct, and came to a head over a television show. I had by then, at fourteen or fifteen, stopped watching all the programs that had held me spellbound in the first two years, with the exception of *Bonanza*, to which I was unnaturally attached. My mother had no objections, except if she had plans to go somewhere, and that, of course, always involved me. On one of those occasions, we would not have gotten back in time to see the show, and I refused to go. My mother tried to force me by pulling me off the bed. In resisting her, I inadvertently kicked her in the chest. It was an awful moment.

Despite the kick, I was not fighting fully. I could not really afford to win. In New Jersey, there were no Madame Pincẓewkis or Madame Friedas or Madame Urbachs. We lived in a neighborhood that might have provided my mother with similar friendships. Quite a few immigrant Eastern European families lived on the block, even if my cousins were second-and third-generation Americans. But with each, there was an obstacle. Mrs. Berger was too young, becoming pregnant with a third child in the middle of that six-year period, by accident, my mother had clarified. I turned becoming pregnant by accident often in my teenage mind, trying to solve the physical problem this presented. Mr. and Mrs. Kafka lived on the same floor with their two large boys; they were observant, leaving *sholokhmones*, a gift basket, on our doormat on Purim. My mother, despite the fact that we practiced none of them, had a sentimental attachment to the religious practices of her childhood, but here it did not become a bond. Madame Lola, in my cousins' building, was too old, and so it went. My mother was a widow among married couples, but also was a much more recent immigrant. When we lived on 51st Street, I never considered dates of arrival to the United States. Several people on the block had been in the camps. Perhaps they had immigrated only twelve or fifteen years before us. At the time, they seemed very different from us, from here, in the way we were not.

Contributing to my mother's isolation was also her occupation. She sewed fur collars and buttons onto winter coats with co-workers, who by this time, were primarily Italian and Spanish-speaking. Once, when she came home from work, she told me that she had been asked by a co-worker to step out of a group photograph. Her tone, quietly resigned, brought me almost to tears. Within her own family, her relationship with the only people with whom she could communicate easily, her sister Hela and brother-in-law Jacques, became tense. Jack, who had been a successful factory, thought being a finisher of ladies' coats was too humble an occupation. He could not understand why my mother consented to work for so little money. We visited them regularly during our years in New Jersey, but my mother felt that she had turned into the poor relative that one wanted to keep at arm's length. When we stayed with them for the first three weeks after our arrival, my mother saw my aunt locking their bedroom door when she went out. I never went to check, but I could feel my aunt's distance. The snobbism was probably reciprocal, since my mother had had access to a life in Paris and Warsaw that glittered in a way that her sister's life in North Bergen, New Jersey did not.

In those years there were some gentlemen callers. The dance partner who had held her in the wrong place, the tall married man, appeared at the door very early one fine morning, to declare his uncontrollable passion. Earlier, in the very beginning of our life on 51st Street, a Mr. Kaplan, a widower and from Kalisz, paid her court. He bought us a record player, and our first three records—B. B. King, *Porgy and Bess*, and Polish polkas—which I still have to this day. This unusual eclecticism speaks well of him in my eyes, but it did not impress my mother, at least not enough. I am not sure what would have impressed her enough. As much as she had wanted my father to be a Mr. Kaplan, someone with a steady salary, be it in a nondescript profession, the man she had lived with had not been Mr. Kaplan. The only time he ever stayed over in our apartment, he was relegated to the couch in the living room, after what I perceived to be tense negotiations. He did not come back. Towards the end of our Weehawken period, she even took some active measures, responding to an ad in the *Forverts*. I went with her, of course, to meet a short pudgy man who lived in Connecticut. For a long time afterward, my mother would joke about his poor manners, referring to him in Polish as *nożki do góry*, little legs up, because of the way he had sat on top of the picnic table, above us, with his legs spread apart, while we sat on the bench below.

To combat her loneliness, my mother took her last great leap. We would move to Los Angeles. The preparations for this momentous journey required that I write, under her dictation, a letter to the ILGWU-AFL/CIO office, asking if there was any work for finishers in LA. We received a postcard in response. All I remember is the salutation: "Dear Sister . . ." Yes, there were jobs to be had in the factories of Los Angeles. My mother, somewhat hesitantly, began to sell our furniture. When the school year was over, and the last item had disappeared, she bought two Greyhound bus tickets. And this is how it came to pass that, on July 3, 1968, a short month after Robert F. Kennedy's assassination, we ended up on the other side of the continent. My mother knew no one personally in our new location, and had only one contact, a friend of her sister, a Mrs. Margulies.

One thing has puzzled me about that trip. Upon arriving in downtown LA, we immediately took the local bus to the Fairfax area, the big Jewish neighborhood of the city at the time. We must have had suitcases with us, but only such that one could carry onto a local bus. Yet in my possession now, fifty years later, are two very heavy fur coats, a Belgian rug, and a couple of heavy linen tablecloths. My mother must have had these items shipped, no longer able to find a friendly basement in New Jersey in which to store our past. I do not remember any of these items in our new home, a humble apartment on Curson Avenue, not far from the very gentle and elderly Mrs. Margulies. Fifty years later, the rug is in my living room, the coats are in my closet, occasionally worn on an especially cold day, and the table cloths appear on the table for a holiday meal. I have inherited.

## Instead of Los Angeles

Years ago, my friend Sarah began to record her elderly mother's reminiscences. Despite her appeals, her mother's story would never extend beyond the year 1933. Every time Sarah urged her to say more, she would simply go back to the beginning and end at the same point. It seemed like a small poem to me, this broken record, but I did not give it much thought beyond the moment I heard it. About two decades later, to my surprise, I bumped into the same phenomenon when Sonja, Pien's daughter, and I began to record Pien's life. Her narration would start to frazzle around 1945, or a couple of years later, when she was still in her early twenties. Each of us had heard many stories of Pien's later life, but never as one chain of events, and it was never to become one. To my even greater surprise, the pattern has repeated in the retelling of my own story. Although all the important decisions of my life occurred after 1968, I cannot tell my story as a continuous tale beyond this point. This is where the chronology ends. It may be that for each of us a certain myth of origins gradually shows its lineaments. After that, we may have many stories, but none that is foundational.

If the myth of origin has a non-negotiable beginning and end, it also sets the stage for what cannot be so easily delimited: the questions, the battles, the regrets embedded in the original narrative. Each of the following essays—"Communism," "Jewish," "Mental Illness," "Money," "Russian Friendships," and "Theological Fragments"—expands on some aspect already present in the chronological tale, trying to stay close to the concrete twists and turns of the biography, but nonetheless taking flight beyond them. In 2018-2020, this is what persisting too long in the same generation looks like to me. The generation in question is that of Eastern European Jews whose twentieth century was marked by migration, war, and more migration. The fact that this description is more characteristic of my parents than of me just means that children do not choose what they inherit. I conclude with "Talking to Myself about Literature," a meditation on the "I" of the memoir and the academic "I," so often intertwined in these pages.

# 2

# Communism

The documents of the Institute of National Memory list all the Communist parties that my father had belonged to: the German Communist Party (the KPD), the French Communist Party (the PCF), and the Polish Communist Party (the PZPR).[1] Since one of its strictly confidential reports lists my father's profession as film actor, the first time I ever heard of it, I allowed myself a modicum of skepticism. In this case, however, all of those party affiliations are undoubtedly correct. In a book memorializing the Jewish combatants in the International Brigades, my father, Yaakov Aronowicz, Yashar (his stage name) appears as already having exhibited Communist sympathies in his late adolescent years, in the German gymnasium in which he completed his studies.[2] As to his membership in the French and Polish Communist parties, that is incontrovertible. He was expelled from France in 1949 for activities relating to the party; the Polish state security services, the source of the list of memberships, would surely not have made a mistake as to whether he belonged to the Polish United Workers Party. Come to think of it, they may have been right about the film acting as well. My mother told me that once when she had asked my father how it had been to kiss women on stage, he had answered that he was so concentrated on the role that he felt nothing, seemingly satisfying her curiosity. Since it is unlikely that passionate kissing played a large role in the Yiddish theater, especially in the high-minded art theater of the Communist variety, maybe he had been not only a stage but also a film actor.

---

1   The files referred to throughout the essays are IPN Bu 0423/3546, dot. 0/Wa WK-9879/13; IPN BU 0423/3548 dot. O/Wa WK-9879/13; IPN BU 1547/84 (EWA I 10519/56) dot.0/Wa WK-9879/13. In addition, I drew on a slim folder containing my parents' requests for a visa abroad, dotted with so many file numbers that I was not able to determine the key ones.

2   Ephraim Wuzeck, *Zikhroynes fun a Botvinist* (Warsaw: Yidish Bukh, 1964), 92-93.

My father, Yashar, right, and Oskar Fessler, left, performing on the Yiddish stage in a purim shpil *Homens mapole* performed in Paris between 1946 and 1949.

My mother, on the other hand, had never been a party member. It is surprising, in fact, how little of the requisite ideology she absorbed. I have mentioned the two summer camps she sent me to in Belgium, after my father died. One was Communist, the other, its ideological nemesis, Zionist. Her reasoning had been that the former was in the mountains and the latter on the beach, providing me with the necessary balance of fresh air. Even more a sign of the lack of reeducation from her petty bourgeois past was that once in Belgium, as I have already relayed, she pleaded with my father to buy the grocery store for sale on the corner of our block. Even I understood that this was a monumental ideological error. My father, of course, proceeded, from Brussels, to set up a business international in scope. It involved the trading of wool between Poland and China. I imagine it was Polish wool. Did Communist China not have sheep? Boris, my father's friend, when I spoke to him about this later, claimed that the business might have worked. It just needed more than the two short years that my father poured into it before his death. The only physical traces of his efforts, an Olympia typewriter with a European keyboard and a used leather satchel containing some hastily scribbled notes, travelled with us to the United States. The debts were left behind. My mother's loyalties were very local, crossing with Communism only by accident.

From another angle, however, my father might himself have conceded to, if not initiated, some frankly bourgeois behavior. How else to explain the Louis XV-style furniture that graced our living room in Poland, originating from the Paris years in the Montmartre apartment, and which also followed us to Brussels? Was the idea that in the new society, everyone would have Louis XV-style furniture? Something like this answer was once given to me by the resident Marxist at the college in which I taught. After he got tenure, he and his wife moved out of their modest digs, buying a house with a swimming pool in the suburbs. We teased him about his bourgeois tastes. He defended himself. The Marxist goal was not to diminish the standard of living but to make a higher one available to all. They were already living in the future. I am not sure that my parents' purchase of Louis XV furniture was so connected to the working out of a dialectic.

I do not, in fact, know what determined my father's choice to become a Communist nor what his thinking on class or anything else was. One might expect that the documents from the Institute of National Memory would yield some hints, even if only through the statements party members were obligated to make. One of the secret reports mentions that my father's official line on political issues remains unknown, since he gave no public speeches either in academic settings or at party meetings, saying very little in department meetings as well. The report appears to relate this lack of ideological clarity to my father's linguistic limitations. Aronowicz's Polish is peculiar, the reporter writes, spoken with a strong accent, with a stutter, as if this were not his native language. It is surprising this is put so delicately, for any native speaker should have been able to detect that my father was not Polish, despite the nationality and citizenship he had acquired. Born in Wilno (Vilnius) when it belonged to the Russian Empire, he spoke Russian, his mother tongue, excellently, as the office spy reported. In any case, my father managed enough Polish to function in his high-level job. My mother said that he had hired a Polish tutor in Warsaw, a young woman with whom he flirted. The flirting did not help. His Polish remained heavily accented, and, according to my mother, incorrect. I myself never noticed the difference between my mother and my father's language at home. It was Polish. Of course, at five or six, I would have been quite incapable of detecting his party line, regardless of his pronunciation.

My father in Otwock, c. 1954.

Like almost everything else I know about my father, the source of what Communism might have represented to him was my mother. Left to her stories alone, I might have surmised that Communism had to do with Yiddish, singing and dancing, books and theater, and risking one's life for someone else's cause. She would often tell me about how they met. Both arrived in Paris in 1933, she from Kalisz, in Central Poland, and he from Berlin. One day, the Kultur Lige, a cultural and social center for the city's Eastern European Jewish immigrants, organized a Yiddish book sale, which coincided with a ball. My mother manned one of the tables. My father came up and invited her to a waltz. That did it—he led so well, she would sigh, claiming decades later that she could never dance with anyone else. Another oft-repeated story involved Yiddish theater. My father acted in the recently organized Paris Yiddish Workers Theater, known by its acronym, PYAT. He would invite my mother when he was not performing. She must have been around twenty in those years. In her later description of their walks at night, Paris, Yiddish culture, love and no money, and my father's panache blended into one inextricable mix, lending her youth its radiant colors. Her judgment of my father's artistic ability was less exalted, although he scored very well in many categories. Acting—not so good. If he was given mostly silent parts, it was for a reason; singing, excellent; Yiddish, excellent, a Vilne Yiddish; I have already spoken about her evaluation of his dancing. The third story, really not a story, was the fact that he left for Spain to join the International Brigades to defend the Republican side. He would write her letters. Few details from them made their way to me, but something of the greatness of that cause must have come through in her telling. I have always been inordinately proud that he went to fight there. And fight he did, in the Thaelman Battalion, and eventually in the Botwin Company.

A friend of my father, Oskar Fessler, described to me one day how they ended up in Spain. He, my father, and another friend, Isa Shapiro, took a bus to the border, three young men off to a war whose brutality none of them suspected at the time, all three of them actors. When I relayed this to a young friend of mine recently, he said, yes, but they were ordered to go by the party. No doubt they were ordered to go. But who could doubt the enthusiasm of the people who went? The Communist Party did not invent Franco and it did not invent Hitler. To have volunteered to fight in Spain was, for a long time, a spot of purity on one's conscience. That purity was marred by the murderous tactics of the Soviet commissars on the ground. But I cannot confuse that with the intentions of those three young men. To decide to risk one's life to stop Hitler and Mussolini remains a choice for good. The irony, of course, is that the Soviet regime, itself so involved in supporting the Republican cause, became very suspicious of the "Spaniards," those who had fought in Spain. In my father's secret police file, his time as a volunteer in Spain seems, along with his long stay in France, to have been reason to watch him carefully.[3] Having strong bonds elsewhere than in Poland cast a shadow on his loyalties.

Going back to my mother's stories about her life in Paris, one might legitimately ask what any of them had to do with Communism. My mother did not make the link. These were stories of her youth and not of Communism. It just so happens that all these events had a link with it. The Kultur Lige had by 1933-1934 been taken over by Jewish Communists, in a fierce battle with the Bundists, Jewish socialists, some of whom were still nursing their wounds sixty

3    For a very good account of the International Brigade volunteers, including their postwar destinies, see Lisa A. Kirschenbaum, *International Communism and the Spanish Civil War: Solidarity and Suspicion* (Cambridge: Cambridge University Press, 2015). On the fear of the "Spaniards," see ibid., 213-215.

years later. But as involved in political struggle as the Jewish Communists were, it so happened that at that time and place their social world was built on book sales and romances, volleyball matches and theater performances, lectures and choirs, language lessons and much else. The Bundists and the Zionists were creating similar social worlds. Before she left Kalisz, my mother had belonged to a Jewish socialist organization, either the Bund or the Poalei Tzion. She never conveyed to me the difference in the political programs, which were significant. For her, all these movements were the communities available in the world in which she grew up, shading into one another in their rebuilding of a Jewish society on a new basis. In Kalisz, she had been among Jewish socialists, in Paris she lived among Communists. It was a matter of chance and location in her case, but her case was not that exceptional.

My desire to reconstruct the atmosphere in my mother's stories led me to investigate the Yiddish theater in Paris, which had been founded under Communist auspices before the war, to revive only for a brief period after the war. By the time I met them, from the mid-nineties to the early 2000s, the few elderly people who had been active in PYAT, the prewar theater, or YKUT, its postwar acronym, were no longer Communists. Spending time with them evoked stories that, just like my mother's, were not specifically about Communism, and yet conveyed a universalism ardently yearned for, and, to a degree, embodied. Oskar Fessler, over eighty at the time, and a very dashing man still, took me to a print shop next to his apartment building so that we could copy some photographs of my father and him on stage. I noticed that the printshop owner was Iranian. After we left, I asked Oskar whether he thought the owner was Jewish. I was trying to figure out whether the Iranian immigration to Paris had been as heavily Jewish as it had been in Los Angeles, although I must admit that I inherited from my mother the automatic impulse to detect Jews, a habit most irritating to my friends. Oskar, a Rumanian Jew, proceeded to remind me sternly of a saying of Levi-Straus engraved on the Musée de l'homme or perhaps the Museum of Ethnography that spoke of being human, exclusively, correcting my deviant interest in Jews. A Yiddish play had launched Oskar's career. (He later became an important theater director in Buenos Aires.) The very photographs we were having copied at the print shop represented Jewish actors in a postwar performance of a purim shpil. a commemoration of the Jewish defeat over the murderous Haman. But we were universalists only, not to be caught in the trap of cultural or ethnic specificities. In that summer, Oskar took me to see a contemporary ballet, explaining to me afterward some of the unusual stage techniques. It was called "Ne m'oublie pas," and I have forgotten neither him nor the human, only human of the Yiddish-tinged culture on the outskirts of which I grew up.

In the early years of my work on Yiddish theater, I also spent a great deal of time with Anna Wilner and her husband Jacques Brudny. They lived in a modest suburb just outside of Paris, on the eighth floor, in an apartment filled with the work of Jewish painters. Look, Anna would point out, that white streak in that dark brown painting, that is hope. Their library was filled with classics, one of which, the works of the great Yiddish poet, Avraham Sutzkever, she wanted to bequeath to me. But her husband, at eighty-eight, could not yet part with any bit of his library. He consoled himself in his increasingly crippling old age by reading German classics in German and Polish classics in Polish, and Russian classics in Russian, languages he had not used in some time. Maybe rereading Yiddish classics in Yiddish was next in line. The lacunae in my reading of the European classics astounded him. What, I had not read *The Magic Mountain*? How could this be? I was ashamed.

Jacques Brudny and Anna Wilner.

On the topic of Communism itself, Anna was still regularly attending to matters in what had been the Jewish Communist headquarters, 14 rue de Paradis, even if Jacques had quietly stopped participating decades earlier, not anti-Communist, just no longer a man with a vision. He used to write essays in the Yiddish press, edit an important Yiddish Communist journal, but now he had lost a way of making the world coherent, he told me. They lived peaceably and lovingly together on these ruins. The only intolerable gesture was to become vocally anti-Communist, as a former friend of theirs had done in his later years. Anna explained that there was such a thing as an ex-Communist honor. She was furious when I had mentioned the friend's name. It was as if to spit on Communism was to spit on the loves that were still evident on their walls and bookcases, a love of the width and breadth of the world. Europe stood for the world, of course, as it did for so many people for at least two centuries. But the point is not that their idea of the world was limited, but that they lived with the ideal of a culture without borders. Anna's defense of Communist honor was also inseparable from the courage Communists displayed during the war. She had gotten her name of Wilner, not only because she, like Jacques, came from Wilno, but also as a member of the Communist Resistance. To have opposed the Nazis at the risk of one's life remained a moment of glory that no betrayal of the Communist ideal, before and after, could sully. Wilner had been her nickname, which she kept it as a surname until she died over sixty years later.

Sentimental nonsense, many would say. Is not focusing on the internationalism and courage of the Communists to turn a blind eye to all the horrors that Communism produced? Since I have written at length elsewhere on the persecution of two famous Soviet Jewish writers, Isaac Babel, and Osip Mandelstam, I am quite informed about the ideological insanity, the terror, the torture that led to these writers' murders, as it led to the murders of so many others. My point in ruminating about my father's participation in the movement was not to hide these realities but to show that they do not cover all that the Communist movement meant, and by a long shot. It is nonetheless true that I had never come close to finding out what my father did in his six years as vice director of imports in the Ministry of Commerce. My mother had no stories. For six years, 1950-1956, the Polish Communist government's very wide net of informers, one hundred fifty thousand by some counts, made fear a constant, daily presence, brutally suppressing real and imagined opposition. At the height of repression, in 1952, there were approximately fifty thousand political prisoners in Poland.

On October 9, 2013, I filed a request to see my father's record, as gathered by the secret police, the UBP. My first encounter with the Institute in which those files were stored was reminiscent of Joseph K.'s forays into the bureaus of Kafka's fiction. In a building, fairly new and ten stories high, in a rather forsaken part of the city, two clerks sat behind windows at opposite ends of the small room into which one entered from the street. After explaining myself in Polish, with great difficulty, I thought I would be led to a waiting room inside. But there was no inside. I stood in that small entrance way until a young woman appeared from one of the ten floors. We sat at a small table in the corner, while she helped me fill out my formal request for documents. She asked me some questions, in an impeccably impersonal tone. Was my father a victim of the Communist repression? He was a Communist himself, I answered. She looked impassively on. I then mentioned that he had been expelled from his job in 1956, with the coming of Władysław Gomułka into power. That lifted an invisible barrier. The Institute of National Memory, it turns out, was established in 1998 to pursue crimes against the Polish nation. At the center of its staff's attention was the Communist regime. Since one of the Institute's missions was not only to research Communist crimes but also to prosecute the guilty parties, had I not thought to mention my father's expulsion, the young lady might have sent me to another part of town, to visit the legal arm of the organization. It seems one was either a victim or a perpetrator. There was no other possibility to understand participation in the Communist regime.

In filling out the forms, I had written down my father's first name and patronymic as Jakub, son of Moshe. (Once I got the files, I noted that my father had given his name as Jakub, son of Michał.) There was no escaping it, another Jewish participant in the Soviet-imposed Communist regime. As I wrote, the small room seemed to fill with silent accusations of Żydokomuna. Even in my short forays into Poland since 2007, it had been impossible not to read or hear about Communism as a Jewish plot to control the Polish nation. Sitting in that tiny space, with thirty kilometers worth of files from the Communist security services stored above my head, I felt accused without having done anything. For some reason, it made me smile to myself, as if I were in on a joke. To have been a Jew in the Communist regime was to make the party too Jewish. Many besides my father were expelled from the party and from the government in 1956 for that reason, and then in 1967 from Communist Poland itself, accused of being a threatening fifth column. But many anti-Communists, as opposed as they were to all things Communist, nevertheless agreed with them that there were too many Jews in the party. This is a very old and oft-repeated story. I have been spared any but second-hand accounts. Inside this building, filling out these forms, I felt that I was both the butt of the joke and the audience uniquely positioned to appreciate its humor.

Ironically, the files I eventually obtained on my father did reflect his Jewish participation in the Communist government. When I read descriptions of the import and export deals he made, it resembles nothing so much as an old-fashioned international Jewish network. My father had lived in many countries, had spoken many European languages well, and had known people in many places. I am sure some of his business contacts were Jews he knew either through the various Communist Parties to which he had belonged in the course of his wanderings, or scattered members of the International Brigades, often Communists as well. What comforts me in this opinion is that my parents' circle, international in its cultural and political aspirations, was socially thoroughly Jewish. When we moved to Brussels, to which my father had previously travelled in his role as vice director of imports, my parents became friendly with the Kalichmans and the Knoblauchs, Jews with whom my father had done business before. The New Man the Polish People's Republic was striving to build relied at least in part, on age-old Jewish networks. Is this Żydokomuna or simply the acknowledgement by the Polish state that it needed people with international contacts, who spoke German, Russian and French well?

A story about ball bearings is simultaneously terrifying and comical. According to another secret report, my father had been put in charge of finding ways to circumvent the capitalist countries' embargo on trade of certain goods with Soviet block-countries. Among those prohibited but necessary goods were ball bearings. As described in the secret file, my father had a contact in Vienna, who had a ball bearing factory in Venezuela. He knew yet someone else who could arrange for a Polish vessel to pick up the ball bearings from South America, a large quantity of them. The informer writes that these methods of doing business had been unknown to the department in charge of international business before. Matters like the purchase of ball bearings were reported anonymously, on sheets stamped "strictly confidential," with all sorts of markings resembling case numbers. Sometimes the state security services decided that no incriminating evidence against the subject of the report had been found. Sometimes, they decided that the information provided should be used as a basis for further investigation. This latter response could lead to charges of treason, as it did in the case of my father and others. Had they been convicted, the punishment would have been prison, and possibly torture and death.

The intent of the surveillance was clearly to ferret out enemies of the state. Looked at from an admittedly great distance, however, many pages in my father's files look like nothing so much as ordinary job evaluations. The Polish informant's top secret information reveals that my father is well-liked in the office, that he has a reputation as a good businessman, that he cooperates with other branches of the Ministry. But he also takes high risks; it is not certain that he always gets the best prices, as in the case of the briquettes of Polish coal he undersold according to many, and maybe some people had profited from the deal under the table. The informant then adds, perhaps not wanting to get

my father into trouble despite the fact that he had to include something negative to be credible, that my father did obtain permission from the Ministry for
that low price. In many respects, the style and intent of the reporting resemble
these kinds of reports everywhere, and most especially the anonymous reporting on fellow workers, encouraged in today's large corporations, supposedly to
improve performance and to get rid of bad apples.[4]

In the case of Communist Poland, there is a kind of grotesque humor in
using the vast resources of the state secret service to evaluate whether a func-
tionary is asking too high or too low a price on a product or how well they speak
the native language. That that humor is inseparable from terror is undeniable,
although how they can coexist, I do not know. I am also not sure at all that
some combination of terror and grotesque humor is missing from today's business world. How can I be saying that? At most, today's anonymously surveilled
employee risks losing a job, not his or her freedom or life. I understand the
difference. It is huge. But it does not take the terror away from losing one's job.
Neither does it take away from the fact that most instances of spying in Poland
did not lead either to imprisonment or death. In all cases of such anonymous
reporting, an enormous apparatus, made to seem rational and necessary, is
brought to bear on something tiny, thus the grotesque, which it can crush with
impunity, thus the terror.

For Communist organizations or governments, the terror involved an
extra flourish. My father, according to a short report, once received a phone call
from England during a departmental meeting. The informant records the brief
conversation: Yes, yes, everyone is fine. No, no, we do not need anything. Don't
send anything. Yes, Hanushka. Is fine. The fact that some version of my name
is mentioned means that it was a personal call. I can feel the effort my father
makes to cut the conversation short. He probably knew that it would appear
suspect. But why, one might ask? It was with someone outside the country, the
nature of whose relationship with my father was not known. Everything has
to be known. I had encountered this when I finally obtained some files on a
Jewish Communist playwright from the French Communist Party archives. He
had asked permission, in the mid-1950s, to travel to Argentina where one of his
plays was being performed on the Yiddish stage in Buenos Aires. Permission
was refused: "Comrade Sloves will be out of our sight for five weeks." My father's

---

4   For one example of these corporate practices, see Jodi Kantor and David Streitfeld,
    "Inside Amazon: Wrestling Big Ideas in a Bruising Workplace," *New York Times*,
    August 16, 2015.

many contacts in many countries, his frequent trips in order to meet with his counterparts personally also put him out of sight of the party. Eventually, a case is built against him and more than a dozen others around business dealings with an Italian named Spartaco Vannoni, the Secretary of the Italian Embassy in Warsaw, who also represented various business enterprises. The charge is spying against the interests of the People's Republic of Poland. The case is eventually dropped, but my father, along with many others, is dismissed from his job all the same.

In reading these files, I do not feel any shame about my father's role in that government. I feel sorrow that this is the order he ended up serving, after all the hope and all the battles waged in good faith. I also wish that he had had either the good sense or the good luck to get out earlier, once he did begin to serve it. But, from the documents I see nothing but someone trying to buy and sell things, with the same panache as he had had as a Yiddish actor. It was considerably more taxing. In the period 1956-1958, photographs reveal that his face has turned into a grim mask. What was he thinking? About this—the one important matter—the documents of the Institute of National Memory say nothing.

My father's passport photo, Warsaw, c. 1958.

My impenitence about his service lays open the possibility that I am a bit of a schizophrenic, exonerating the Jewish Communists I have known personally, all the while opposing the Communist state and the Communist Party that they served. It is indeed possible that I am like one of those children who refuse to own up to the crimes of their fathers, an admittedly much paler version of

Joseph Goebbels's daughter, who insisted until the end of her life that her father had been a good man. But my father did not shoot the wretches in the dungeon, as the Soviet poet Sergei Esenin wrote, and he did not spy on anyone. He bought ball bearings, and sold Arabian horses. My mother did get some beautiful Italian silk blouses out of it. But this is the ordinary stuff of business exchange, as old as the world.

\*\*\*

Kees Bolle, my teacher, once told me that I had chosen to study the history of religions because, like him, I had had a father with a lifelong devotion to the socialist vision and, like him, I had seen it fail. At face value, this seems most improbable. My father died when I was eight, taking Communism with him. I could hardly have comprehended its basic principles from my mother, whose preoccupations lay elsewhere. Besides, nothing of that introductory class in the history of religions, on mythology, bore the slightest connection to the socialist movement. I had been so excited by that first lecture, in the spring of 1972, that a friend seated next to me was moved to prophetic utterance: "You will write your dissertation on this." Since the contents of that first class have long since dissipated into unintelligible fragments, it is not at all clear what "this" referred to, although I am convinced that I have written on nothing but "this" ever since.

But surfaces are surfaces. Kees did not mean that I chose to study religion because I had been influenced by Communist ideology. Religion, I learned from him, is the very opposite of ideology, what ideology is not. It is, in its quite diverse manifestations, a vision which organizes the life of a given community. Available only indirectly, its many expressions include "beliefs," without being contained in a list of them. In fact, Kees spoke of religion much like Charles Péguy, the French philosopher and poet whom I began to read a bit later, who called the Dreyfus affair a fine example of a religious phenomenon in the modern world. When it truly functions, religion gives shape to everything there is: friendships, occupation, family relations, education, art, "religion," science. That a vision can be reified, becoming a crude weapon with which to beat political opponents in order to maintain or increase the power of one's group is also the sorry state of human affairs. Péguy characterized this inevitable transformation in a famous sentence. "Everything begins in mystique and ends in politique." Yep. That contrast is what I wanted to study and, accordingly, my dissertation bore the title "Freedom from Ideology." I was ambitious.

Given the current and not so current climate in the United States, one might think that Communism represented only *politique*, iron-clad ideology, skipping the life-giving aspect altogether. But I know it was not that, and many people who grew up with socialist or Communist parents know it as well. Besides my mother's stories, I have my own memories of a liveliness, a conviviality around our table, and of friendships my father had made—in Spain, in the slave labor camp, on the Yiddish stage, all bound by a Communist commitment—which survived his death. These friends, and others whom I met later, had a spark, a human warmth that could not have been absent from the Communist movement they joined. These people were the Communist movement. My own encounter with them would not fit properly into an official document, and yet it too is a real indicator of what that movement was, perhaps a deeper indicator.

Very recently, a friend sent me a very short excerpt from an interview with the French writer Robert Antelme, whose book about Buchenwald, published in 1947, has become a classic.[5] When asked about the essential lesson of his experience of Buchenwald, he replied that the German concentration camps revealed, in an extremely magnified way, the evil inherent in man's exploitation of the work of man.[6] Sounding so unlike the richly textured and reflective voice that I remember from *L'Espèce humaine*, Antelme, in this interview, seems to be alluding to a Communist slogan, very common at the time, equating capitalism and fascism. Nazi concentration camps, in this reading, were but a mirror of what our economic system does to human relations in normal life, but as if grotesquely enlarged. To fight against this exploitation was the true legacy of the camps. And yet, even if Antelme's sentence sounds like a political slogan, and a Communist one at that, the experience of exploitation to which it referred is not a slogan. Millions of people rose up, adhering in one way or another to the Communist movement, because of that experience of exploitation, in the hope of never having to be humiliated again, never having to be made into objects for someone's else's profit. Sometimes, a slogan, in its woodenness and inadequacy, can nonetheless refer to a profound living source beneath. Communism, even in the way it was transmitted to me as a child, was both the wooden slogan and the living source beneath.

---

5   Robert Antelme, *The Human Race*, trans. Jeffrey Haight and Annie Mahler (Evanston: Marlboro Press, 1998).

6   https://fresques.ina.fr/jalons/fiche-media/InaEdu07042/robert-antelme-la-littera-ture-sur-les-camps-de-concentration-audio-audio-audio-audio.html#transcription.

We all know, however, that the same hope, the same concern for the dignity of the human being, led to the most terrifying results—the death of millions, not only in Soviet slave labor camps but also in the torture chambers of the prisons, and the forced confessions of the show trials. Even if Communism as a movement cannot be reduced to an ironclad set of principles, expressed in slogans, it nonetheless had something in it that very quickly turned it into a murderous weapon. The seed of its destructiveness is, I think, well conveyed in the memoir of Artur London, *On Trial*, in which the author recounts his sudden imprisonment, torture and trial for treason in the Communist Czechoslovakia of the early 1950s, around the same time as my father was figuring out how to buy ball bearings for the People's Republic of Poland.[7]

London was an old time Communist, twenty-two years in the party by the time he came to be a highly placed official in postwar Czechoslovakia. He, along with the thirteen other Communists put on trial on charges of espionage and treason, were all veterans of the International Brigades, most of them Jewish. For all of them, party discipline was central. In Spain, London had in fact been in charge of disciplining the Communist volunteers. He describes it in his memoir as a necessity of war, but also as a way of instilling the party spirit, of rehabilitating people. In his eyes, it was very different from what party discipline meant in his own trial and that of his fellow prisoners.[8] Nonetheless, in both cases, obedience to the party was a fundamental dictate, ensuring the victory of the Revolution. The party, representing the vanguard of history saw into the workings of the dialectic. It knew the way forward. Artur London's wife, Lise Ricol, a lifelong Communist like himself, once claimed that doubting the party was the first sign that one had stopped being a Communist.[9]

The party's insistence on embodying a supposedly objective truth made for the ultimate defeat and destruction of the prisoners on trial. Absolute obedience was a necessary offshoot, for what moral ground can one stand on if one opposes the truth? As London describes it, party discipline in the show trial required far more than subordinating one's own opinion to that of the leadership. It meant accepting that one's own particular experience of the world had neither inherent worth nor inherent reality.[10] If the party maintains that London had survived Mauthausen because he collaborated with the Gestapo,

---

7   Artur London, *On Trial*, trans. Alastair Hamilton (London: Macdonald & Co., 1970).
8   Ibid., 76-77, 111.
9   Ibid., 17.
10  "'Every fact, every action,' they told me, 'must be judged objectively in the report. Its subjective side will be appreciated later.'" (Ibid., 111) "Everything we had done was

then the fact that he was part of the Communist resistance in that very harsh German slave camp, and that others could corroborate it, matters not in the slightest. It is merely "subjective." Only the party's view is "objective."[11] The terms subject and object are out of joint. There was nothing subjective about London's role in the Communist Resistance. There was nothing objective about the party interrogators' claim that he had been a collaborator. But if dismissing individual perspective and experience in view of the pronouncements of the party was the very proof of loyalty to the Communist cause, the consequence was extreme. In the show trials, it was not enough to accept sacrificing yourself for the needs of the party. In that case at least some members of the party would know that you were innocent, even if they condemned you to death for treason, acknowledging your personal reality, even if only in private and face to face. The sacrifice required in the show trial, however, was to erase your personal reality altogether, leaving in its place only party dictates. There was no private wink because there was no personal reality. You were guilty if the party said you were guilty.

All fourteen of the accused eventually confessed. Of course, they were tortured through sleep deprivation, forced walking in their prison cells day and night, beatings and hunger. But they were also tortured by their own understanding of what was required of them. An interrogator appealed to London's conscience by pointing to the example of one of the other prisoners who had already confessed. "By confessing he has shown that he still has a spark of true communism in him, and that we only have to blow on it to revive it."[12] The logic is absurd. London was being asked to give up on the very idea of a personal conscience at the same time as he was asked to act on it. Even fifteen years later, London feels compelled to respond to the accusation that he should not have confessed with a revealing retort: "I must emphasize the fact that I was in the hands of the Party. . . . How can one fight if the enemy are the Party and the Soviet advisers, and any struggle is regarded as a struggle against the Party and the Soviet Union?"[13] Although his memoir describes the physical torture in detail, it is not to that he appeals as an excuse for having capitulated. He had been tortured by the Nazis and had not capitulated.

---

judged in the light of the immediate international situation, according to the political standards in force at that moment in the USSR." (Ibid., 114)

11  Ibid., 142.
12  Ibid., 145.
13  Ibid., 436.

I would submit that while we still feel a mixture of bewilderment and horror in reading accounts such as London's, we become tongue-tied when asked what it is that is violated when we become a mere vessel for the "objective" truth. The word "soul "might come to mind to indicate the violated entity but it is suspect, as if by using it we were refusing the latest scientific findings about the material world, insisting on bringing in a dubious and empirically unverifiable spirit. As to the word "self," it too is on trial, if we mean by it an independent entity not entirely the product of external forces. The digital micro-targeting of voters and consumers, for instance, intended to shape and control their choices, only proves the point since it is so often pronounced successful. But if we do not have a word to describe what is violated in a case such as London's, has anything been violated? We are left with the vision of ourselves as malleable atoms, neurons, molecules, genes. Torture is a very crude instrument to instill or extract the "objective truth," to be sure, but, in principle, insisting that we have an inside that one kills by invading it is now labeled romantic nonsense. Why use torture when we have better, gentler means of inserting and extracting?

You are exaggerating, I hear someone saying, maybe me. Only academics talk like this. Normal people do not go in for such mental contortions. They speak about nothing but the self, taking classes to assert it, doing yoga and meditation to calm it, priding themselves on being savvy consumers, occasionally asking to have their brains frozen in the hope of eternal selfhood, writing memoirs if cryonics does not appeal. I do not find in any of these activities proof of the continued viability of the self, either as a concept or as a reality. In the face of a barrage of techniques meant to read our minds, our faces, our genes, our futures, our pasts, our presents, the claim to an experience accessible only from the inside, impermeable to the outside observer, is increasingly undone by data, huge and huge reams of it. We are our data. They can be harvested, analyzed, manipulated. Algorithms tell us who we are.

The religious dimension of our time, I would contend, lies in works that both reflect the phenomenon of the vanishing self and stimulate us to refuse to cede it. In London's memoir most striking in this regard is his account of how, forced to walk day and night in his cell, he keeps on recalling the faces of the people he had known, speaking to them out loud, as if they were present. "So, between interrogations my cell became an asylum where I met my companions. I must have talked aloud for my door opened and an angry warder said: 'Stop telling that nonsense to the walls!'"[14] London's attempt to conjure

---

14  Ibid., 152.

up these images needs to be seen against the performance required of him and others during the show trials. It was not enough for the accused to read fabricated accounts of their lives to the assembled public. They had to memorize them, as if to displace or erase memory itself.[15]

I seem to have gotten carried far from where I began. All I really wanted to say is that I have been captivated not only by the life-giving vision that shapes every society but also by the disappearing conduit of that life-giving vision, the self, that seems in so many ways to be a mark of ours. In this long exegesis of Kees's enigmatic statement about our respective fathers, socialism, and religion, made so long ago, I recognize that having had a father both devoted to and defeated by the Communist vision has not been indifferent to my choice of concerns.

*** 

In the summer of 1995, I met Gérard Frydman. He must have been around seventy at the time, vigorous, gruff, and fifty years later, still a keeper of the flame for the Paris Yiddish theater in which he had acted in the years immediately following the war. He and some other youths had represented, for the older generation, the hope for Yiddish culture after the murder of the vast majority of its speakers. Gérard had gathered a trove of documents, some of which he had archived with a national library of the arts in Paris, and some of which he kept at home. He had known my father as Yashar, his stage name, and like all those who were still alive and who remembered him, he received me very warmly. One afternoon, seated at his living room, I was babbling excitedly about the possibility of reconstructing the mentality of that period through the documents he was providing me, when he interrupted me abruptly. "You are seeking for your father but you will never find him."

During the years that I worked on the Yiddish theater in Paris, I heard many similar remarks. That is, friends and acquaintances saw in my choice of topic a way to breach the distance caused by my father's early death, an attempt to reestablish a lost intimacy. Most of these commentators, unlike Gérard, looked positively at these efforts, necessary and important psychological work, in their view. Touching, they claimed. It is a sign of my obtuseness that I was surprised by this every time, and a little offended. I am trying to understand

---

15  Ibid., 249, 251, 271.

Jews in the twentieth century, distinguish between ideology and religion, and all you see is my search for my missing father?

But if concerning my scholarly work, there is some excuse for finding such comments misplaced, surely in what purports to be a memoir of sorts one does not need to ride the high horse of intellect. One can admit what every sentence betrays, that one is a lowly seeker of a missing father, joining so many others whose fathers disappeared, in one way or another. Nothing shows this more than my choice of Artur London's autobiographical account as a conduit to the destructive seed of Communism. There are so many others that would have made my point about the disappeared self.[16] But London's profile, unlike that of many others, resembles that of my father to a remarkable degree.

The list of similarities is long. London and my father joined the Communist movement as adolescents. Both fought in Spain as volunteers in the International Brigades. During the Second World War, both were interned as Communists rather than as Jews in German slave labor camps, although not in the same one. After the war, each returned to France, resuming their prewar Communist activities. As the Soviet Union's influence extended over Eastern Europe, the Communist leadership recruited both men to serve as high-ranking officials in the newly established Communist states. While my father and mother went to Poland, London and his family moved to Czechoslovakia, where he served in the Ministry of Foreign Affairs. After a brief tenure in their respective ministries, both men were accused of espionage against the party and the state, although only London was subsequently tried and convicted. Both eventually left for the West, where they spent their last years. They had probably known each other in their various peregrinations in service to the Communist cause.

But London, unsurprisingly, is not my father. For one, he became an apparatchik much earlier, training as a cadre in a Soviet leadership school in the early 1930s, and spending his time in Spain as a Soviet representative in charge of Communist discipline.[17] My father, in the meantime, fought in the infantry in the horrendous battle of Guadalajara, and eventually became an entertainer for the troops.[18] The other difference, at least as far as I can see, is that my father

---

16  A brilliant analysis of the erasure of the self occurs in the well-known work of Hannah Arendt. See, for example, "Ideology and Terror: A Novel Form of Government," *The Review of Politics* 15, no. 3 (July 1953): 303-327.

17  London, *On Trial*, 52-53.

18  David Diamant, *Combattants juifs dans l'armée républicaine espagnole, 1936-1939* (Paris: Éditions Renouveau, 1979), 109. This is an expanded version of the prior

remained a Jewish Communist, Yiddish-speaking, participating in Jewish communal activities, Communist-led to be sure (to each his *shtiebl*), retaining his Hebrew stage name of Yashar (Upright) even in some official Polish documents, and marrying a Polish Jewish woman who insisted on having him buried in a Jewish cemetery. Perhaps London had been Yiddish-speaking as well, but this never appears either in his own account or that of others. He changed his name to Gérard, which he refers to as his Christian name, a mere idiomatic expression, but also a sign of the desire to blend in more easily with the mainstream culture. His wife, the above mentioned Lisa Ricol, was from a Spanish Catholic family, whose father was a fervent Communist, but whose mother retained her loyalty to the Catholic tradition. In *On Trial*, when London mentions the antisemitism of his interrogators, he treats it as a reminder of an identity that for a true Communist is completely incidental. The focus on his Jewish origins offends him deeply because, whether positively or negatively viewed, being Jewish should have become totally irrelevant.[19]

London's relationship to his wife figures prominently in his memoir. A second generation Communist, her allegiance to the party was so strong that when she heard her husband of many years read his confession of guilt on the radio, the only explanation she had received for his sudden arrest, she immediately wrote a letter to the Central Committee. In it, she said that although she loved her husband, nothing was higher than the party. Since her husband had betrayed it, she would be seeking a divorce.[20] There was not a shred of opportunism in her intention. Her whole life had been obedience and devotion to the party, which she had proved at great risk to herself during the war. She had met her husband in the Soviet Union in the early thirties, both there in service to the cause. As she saw it, the break-up of her marriage was simply the sacrifice that was required of her at this moment. It was difficult but she was up to the task. Later, when she finds out that London is innocent, she moves heaven and earth to help him. But that first reaction is telling. London does not blame her for it. He had expected it, and continues to respect her integrity, even as he wishes he could make known to her the real circumstances.

I cannot imagine for a moment my mother acting like Lise Ricol-London. Had my father been thrown in prison on charges of treason for his dealing with Spartaco Vannoni, and had my mother been given permission to visit him, she

---

Yiddish publication *Yidn in Shpanishn Krig 1936-1939* (Pariz: Yidish Bukh, 1967), 143-144.

19  London, *On Trial*, 50.

20  Ibid., 322.

would have made a scene. Again, he did not listen to her. Had he only followed her advice, he could have avoided the mess he was in, not to mention the mess he had created for everyone else. I base this imaginary scenario on the many bits of "advice discarded" she would recite to me long after my father was dead. She had told him not to register as a Jew when the Germans required it after occupying France but, no, he had not listened. She had urged him to tear up his passport when their train was suddenly stopped in Germany on the way to the Soviet Union, on June 22, 1941, the date of the German invasion of the Soviet Union, but, no, he had shown it to the official requesting it. A miracle that they ever made their way back to Paris! She had begged him to buy that grocery store on the corner of their street in Brussels, but, no, he had to trade in international wool etc. . . . As I write this, I hear the reproaches Sheyne Shendl makes to her husband Menahem Mendl in the Yiddish writer Sholem Aleichem's stories, which just proves that great fiction both reflects and shapes our expressions.[21] In both cases, a practical woman tries to redress the incorrigible *luftmentsch* she married, to no avail.

But as grating as my mother's reproaches must have sounded to my father, as they did even to me when I heard them after the fact, my mother would never have written to the Central Committee of the Communist Party either to request or announce her divorce. What party? It is not that my mother was unsympathetic to the ideals that motivated my father. She had no beef with Communism. Utterly foreign to her would have been subordinating her feelings for my father to a larger cause. She felt what she felt and that was the end of the story. Lise and Artur London might have had a happier union but my father's marriage to my mother made of his Communist allegiance a less well-aligned affair, a situation from which I have undoubtedly profited.

Yes, but did my father think like Artur London and countless other Communists that the party represented the vanguard of history, its pronouncements the only objective reading of the moment? Why would he have been the exception? Boris told me that once when my father came back to Paris on a furlough from his military service in Spain they had walked and talked for hours, my father very agitated about some of what he had witnessed. I had the strong sense that these were ethical issues they discussed long into the night but Boris was not more explicit and at twenty I was too young even to know what to ask. Gérard Frydman was right. I will look for my father but I will never find him.

---

21 Sholem Aleichem, *The Adventures of Menahem-Mendl*, trans. Tamara Kahana (New York: Putnam, 1969).

# 3

# Jewish

## Names

I had said earlier that our address in Warsaw was almost as firmly lodged in my memory as my own name. The problem is that my own name is not as firmly lodged as one might expect. In a copy of my birth certificate that I recently obtained from Poland, my name appears as Anna Katarzyna Aronowicz. I knew that my mother had contemplated naming me Katarzyna, but I had not realized that she had made it official. When, for years, I called myself Annette C. Aronowicz, I imagined that the C. was a kind of extra flourish, giving me the appearance of having a middle name, like my American peers. Anna, on the other hand, was not a surprise. My mother had told me that she named me in honor of her niece, my American cousin Anne, whom everyone called Haney. Haney had come to visit my parents in that legendary apartment in Montmartre in 1949. She would write to her soon-to-be husband every day and wash her stockings every night. In my mother's eyes, this combination of romance and practicality boded well, and so Anna I became.

Clearly, my mother was not following the custom of naming only after dead relatives, and most particularly deceased grandparents. Maybe she had embraced the notion that building the New Man, the task set for my father in Communist Poland, required breaking the cycle of history. My mother spoke only with emotion about her father's practice of blessing the heads of his children at the Passover seder, or of carrying her mother's prayer book to the synagogue every Shabbat. But this was the once upon a time of fairy tale. The modern way required something else. She liked the sound of Anna Katarzyna. In passing, it must be said that it had a properly Polish ring, almost a double saint's name, not quite at the level of Mary, mother of God, but close. Aronowicz, our last name, certainly put an abrupt halt to that kind of free association. This seems to contradict how I have described my mother earlier, insisting on reburying my father in a Jewish cemetery, and her very strong sense of the line separating Pole from Jew. The tugs and pulls were the tugs and pulls of the time, the desire to live in the big bright world and the habit of not being of it. With a name like Anna Katarzyna, I might very well have lost the tug and pull myself, but much intervened.

In the first place, no one ever called me by that name. In my childhood, I was always Anulka, Anulek, Anulinka, the last one more rarely used as the suffix was Russian. These were all diminutives but I never responded to another name until we moved from Poland. I was Anulka. In Brussels, I have no idea what I was called in my first year in elementary school. I should check if Belgium at the time required parents to name children according to an officially sanctioned list, as was the case in France, but even if they did not, Anulka Aronowicz would not have been my name in a Belgian classroom of 1958. In second grade, an enterprising teacher changed my name to Annette. What led to this fateful decision, I do not remember. The name has stuck ever since. To this day, I consider it a bit arbitrary, but what can I do? I cannot suddenly start asking friends and strangers to call me Anulek. My father died the year of my new name and so I do not know if he would have switched. But my mother did not until we were already in the States. When I turned twelve or so, she decided I was Anet, stressing the first syllable instead of the second. She did not directly address me that way often. As she grew older and especially in her later years, it is I who developed a diminutive for her—Pussykata, I would call her, polonizing the word. Anet and Pussykata we became.

The one stable element in these permutations remained my last name, Aronowicz. It was endangered only once. When my mother became a US citizen, she took that opportunity to change her name to Arnold. It was easier to pronounce, she explained. Since I was still a minor, I was expected to follow suit but I categorically refused, insisting on getting naturalized on my own the following year, when I would turn sixteen. My mother was furious, claiming that we would now have two separate last names, and how would that look? But none of the usual weapons had any effect. Aronowicz I remain.

I did not like the name Arnold. Even now, when I see it engraved on her tombstone, I react as if there had been a bureaucratic error. She was Różka Aronowicz or Różka Sieradzka, her maiden name, never becoming the American person, Rose Arnold. Yet the name does express her choices, not only her desire to shed a painful past, perhaps, but also her visceral fear. Once, in a strange reversal, when we were on a shopping expedition in Los Angeles, I tried to explain in bits of Polish that bargaining on price with a clerk in a large department store was an inappropriate use of her talents. In response, she furiously whispered back that I should stop speaking Polish because it would indicate to the people around us that we were Jewish. When she had the breakdown that led to her first stay in a psychiatric ward, it was because she imagined that the morgues in LA were crematoria, and she had come to look for me. Arnold was a very thin protection, no protection at all really. But she was right. It did become easier for many people to pronounce her name.

As a postscript to this story about names, on a recent visit to Poland, I attempted to find my grandfather's grave. I had never known whether my mother's father had died before or during the war. My father's family had lived in Lithuania, but in Poland I could at least hope to find out about this grandfather. In the one photograph I have of him, from 1933, he looks to be around sixty, his beard white, his face still smooth. In the genealogical center adjacent to the Warsaw Jewish Historical Institute, a helpful person found evidence that he had died in the ghetto of Łódź. Once in Łódź, I found another helpful person, who located the record pertaining to his death. He died of typhus on January 27, 1942, and was buried in the New Jewish Cemetery, section G.VI, number 217.

This cemetery turned out to be huge. In the older part, rows upon rows of tombstones, of uneven sizes, many with beautiful carved images, had inscribed upon them the names, significant dates, and relationships of the Jewish denizens of Łódź, this one-time hub of manufacturing and industry. The newer side, a huge, flat field, contained the remains of those Jews who had died or been murdered during the Nazi occupation, prior to the policy of deportations to death camps. Here and there, family members, usually from Israel, had recently erected tombstones. For the most part, though, the field remained a vast homogeneous space, all the graves unmarked. An attendant accompanied me through the poorly delineated rows, wild grass having grown over the narrow paths in many places. When we located G.VI, number 217, I indicated to the attendant that I would be able to find my way back myself. I did not want to do anything in his presence, not even the laying of the pebbles, which I picked up here and there on the way. As to flowers, they were everywhere, small yellow and blue ones, quite beautiful and wild.

Upon returning to the United States, I received a message from the helpful woman in the Łódz Jewish Community Center. She had found yet more information about my grandfather. Before the war, he had remarried and had had another family. This in itself was not implausible. My grandmother had died much before the war, in 1923. But the new information had his date of remarriage precede by far my grandmother's death. There was another Israel Sieradzki. But which was which? I did not know my grandfather's full name, which would have included his patronymic. My mother had given me only Israel, a very common first name; Sieradzki, his last name, was also very common in that region. Distinguishing between several Israel Sieradzkis required the father's father name, the patronymic. The grave upon which I had laid the pebbles was the grave of Israel Meir ben Icek Sieradzki. I may have found the right grave or may have found that of another person, very deserving of the attention I tried to bestow on it.

These missing patronymics bring us back to Anna Katarzyna. I was not given a Hebrew name, as a double to the civil one, the accepted custom in modern times. I became aware that a Hebrew name was needed in mid-adulthood, only when my mother got very sick. Wanting to ask for the traditional blessing for the sick, the "misheberakh," recited during the synagogue service, I named myself Hannah, my namesake's Hebrew name. But I also needed my mother's Hebrew name, as well as the name of her father, for another ritual occasion. I suspect from the way she answered my query, that she did not remember hers either, simply turning Rose into Shoshanah, the way I had turned Anna into Hannah. But with her father and mother's name she did not hesitate. They were Israel and Esther. There was no translation to be done. They had only these names. At the time, I did not know enough to ask for the grandparents' patronymics. They were not necessary for the ritual of asking for the blessing. I also doubt that my mother would have remembered. She had never mentioned her grandparents. Given that she was the ninth child in her family, they were probably long gone by the time she was born. I was surprised to discover, through a recently acquired copy of my father's birth certificate, that my mother had been correct about my father's father Hebrew name, Moshe, as was inscribed on my father's tombstone. I had thought at the time that maybe she had simply made it up, as I did mine.

This meditation on names is recent, as is my searching for official documents and graves. No doubt it is a function of aging, seeking a context in which to situate one's life. An additional feature is also at play, however. What lay before the Second World War seemed to me until relatively recently as far back in time as the Book of Genesis. One could not find out what happened to those aunts in my mother's few photographs. It was a practical impossibility, coexisting with an imperative. One should not seek to know, as if the moral enormity were the only surviving fact. Having been to various Jewish institutions in Poland, some of which arose in the immediate aftermath of the war, I realize now that my mother, upon her return to Poland in 1950, could have gotten some details about her family, which camps, which ghetto, dates of death. She did know about what happened to my father's mother and one of his sisters. Someone my parents knew had reported to them in person that they had been hacked to death in Wilno. I am almost sure, however, that she did not go the Jewish Historical Institute in Warsaw, or if she did, that she did not make these sorts of inquiry. She knew that the sisters and brothers who had remained in Poland were gone, and there was nothing to talk about. I never found this curious, even in adulthood. The past was unreachable, totally unreachable. It was almost a mark of honor to leave it that way. Bringing it into history was to diminish it.

Sixty, seventy years after the war, many besides myself trek to cemeteries in countries to which they have no immediate connection, and reconstruct elaborate genealogies going back centuries based on internet data bases. I have not sought out such ancestral lines, as if my heritage were precisely other than blood and soil. I would root another way. But blood and soil—for what else are genes and ancestral homes but blood and soil?—have a pull despite me, and to my great astonishment. After all, I was born to a Communist father and to a mother who named me Anna Katarzyna, both in their own way lodging me in the universal, away from any particularism of birth and place. That they were also Yaakov bar Moshe and Dora, and Różka bat Israel and Esther should have been an accident of history. To my great good fortune, those names and patronymics bespeak a twice millennial tradition that imagined a mankind rising above blood and soil, although that imagination often stalled. To rediscover my roots is to affirm that one can be deeply planted in a particular people, while chafing against a merely tribal loyalty.

## Return

I have already mentioned that my childhood was devoid of Jewish rituals and even of a soupçon of knowledge about Jewish texts. It was not, however, altogether devoid of Jewish languages. Having gone to a Jewish elementary school in Kalisz, my mother had learned enough Hebrew to join in lustily when we, very rarely, attended a synagogue service after coming to the United States. My mother's mother had been unusually devout, perhaps also accounting for my mother's fondness for long-buried Hebrew words and melodies. As for my father, I do not recall anything linking him with Hebrew, other than his stage name, Yashar, and the inscription on his tombstone, although my mother claimed that it was among the languages he knew. Yiddish, on the other hand, was a strong if peripheral presence. It was the language my parents spoke when they first met, at the Kultur Lige in Paris, since my mother did not speak Russian and my father did not speak Polish. Oskar Fessler, the theater director and fellow fighter in Spain, maintained that my father had learned to speak Yiddish in Berlin so that he could perform on the Yiddish stage, an important vehicle for communicating the Communist message. If so, my father must have learned shades of it that went beyond dialectical materialism, given his successful courtship of my mother. It surprised me to hear that the beautiful Yiddish my mother said he spoke was a secondary acquisition. It is entirely possible, however, that a middle-class family like my father's would already have been speaking Russian at home. In a parenthetical aside, I must say that Russian had a very powerful presence for my own mother, who chose to take with us on our voyage to America the collected works of Pushkin and two volumes of Gogol, beautifully bond, in a language she neither read nor understood. I studied Russian all through my undergraduate years at UCLA, loyal to those Soviet volumes, as if they, and not the many Yiddish classics I have come to read since, held the key to my history.

Yiddish, however, was always in my peripheral hearing, even if by the time they were in Poland my parents rarely, if ever, spoke it to each other and even if it was never a medium of exchange with me during the Warsaw years. At some point, in Brussels and New Jersey, my mother did teach me some Yiddish songs. Over the smoked white fish she would occasionally purchase for Friday nights, or over the obligatory chicken soup, she would occasionally intone "Freytig bay der nakht iz yedener yid a maylekh" (Friday evening every Jew is a king), a stand-in for the melodies accompanying traditional Shabbat rituals, which made no appearance at our table, not even the lighting of Shabbat candles, although, mysteriously, I have inherited from our household a set of old copper Shabbat candle sticks. At other occasions, she would take the time to teach me classic Yiddish lullabies. My education in Yiddish did not go beyond this point until much, much later, and yet I know that Yiddish was more present than these details reveal. Even in Poland, in our apartment, my parents' friends listened to recordings of the great Yiddish standup comics Dzigan and Schumacher. I understood not a word, but when, a lifetime later, I bought some recordings of my own, those ridiculous and so human intonations were so familiar that it is as if I were born listening to them, even though I had to reconstruct very painstakingly the meaning of the words.

In fact, I had heard Yiddish often, already in Brussels, but especially in the New Jersey years. It was the language my mother must have used with Madame Pinczewski and Madame Frieda, at least some of the time. It was the language she used with her sister and brother-in-law and their friends. It was the language I overheard in her phone conversations with her more recent LA acquaintances. A phrase she used over and over in one exchange stays in my mind so many years later. *A gemein shtick.* She had already told me in Polish or French about the cruel tricks of one of her bosses or co-workers. To this day, I ponder the exact meaning of the phrase while knowing perfectly well what she meant.

Yes, Yiddish was present, but it could not by itself, through this very thin if pervasive layer, account for the steps I took as an adult to retrieve what was missing. Perhaps my mother's stories about the concentration camps played a more crucial role. Through who knows which processes, I came to associate being Jewish not with being a victim, but with preferring being a victim to being the perpetrator. I knew then that Jews did not literally choose to be victims, and I know now that their victimhood has led to the current refusal to become victims again, with all the price this exacts on the good I so cherished as a young person, and which I still do. But in my child's mind it was enough that Jews did not commit those terrible deeds my mother described. It was weakness as moral decency, not decency as second best for not having been able to be the perpetrators instead. Yes, yes, I know, how naïve. I insist, however, that I was onto something. It just needs to be better phrased, or better yet, better lived. Is it sentimental to think that the rhythms of Yiddish expressed this very unheroic ethos? Probably. But then, maybe Yiddish speakers had read the great rabbinic authority, Maimonides. "The rule is that he [the Torah sage] should be among the pursued and not the pursuers, among those who accept humiliation but not among those who humiliate others."[1]

The equivalence I drew between *yiddishkeyt* and *menschlekhkeyt*, between being Jewish and being a decent human being was, I repeat, accompanied not only by a total ignorance of any specific Jewish content but also by an ignorance that such a content existed. In Weehawken, several of my little Jewish class-mates brought disturbing details to my attention. Red-haired Sharon Perlman, with that know-it-all air of a sixth grader, told me once as we were walking back from school that we Jews do not eat meat with milk. I quickly rushed home to tell my mother of the nonsense I had just heard only to find that my mother

---

1    Rabbi Moses ben Maimon, *Mishneh Torah*, Hilchot De'ot 5:13.

sided with Sharon Perlman. Another time, Barbara Berger, sitting on the stoop of our apartment building, greeted me with the taunt that we were not good Jews because we did not have a mezuzah on our door post. I sputtered with great passion that we were better Jews than she and her family were, although the evidence I used to back this up escapes me. Once again, my mother sided with the opposition. A mezuzah soon appeared on our door post.

Many years later, a mezuzah graces the front door of my dwelling. It indicates the reversal of my childhood hauteur towards all those benighted practices, although this by no means indicates that I have embraced them in my daily life. I am like a Communist fellow traveler, admiring but not a card-carrying member of the party. The insistence on fellow traveling expresses my loyalty to the universalism of my youth, which I am by no means interested in discarding. Since there is no way to express linearly how this reversal that is not a reversal occurred, perhaps some moments on the path will suggest the heart of things.

In the summer of 1974, I went off to France with the intention of spending my life in the company of an aspiring shepherd from a bourgeois family. For all sorts of reasons, I returned to the States not long afterward, and beginning graduate school, I started to study Hebrew. I did not need it for my language exams, nor for my future studies, for which I was taking Old Church Slavonic, which on top of my years of Russian, would have opened up a research path. I certainly did not take it with the idea of visiting Israel. It wasn't part of the coloring of the Jewish world I inhabited as a child. I took it because I wanted to learn to pray in a Jewish way. Maybe having come so close to being an assistant to a French shepherd, I needed some identifying sign, some mark on my fore-head. But the immediate cause of my desire to learn Hebrew was Primo Levi's *Survival in Auschwitz*, bequeathed to me by a fellow student, next to whom I sat in the UCLA research library for some months. We would occasionally exchange thoughts about this or that, in the middle of plunging into our respective dictionaries, as we were both translating some texts. One day, he brought the book and admonished me to read it. Completely tattered, it now sits on my bookcase next to a much newer edition.

*If This Is a Man*, the original Italian title, is one of the books I know nearly by heart. It is a good book to know that way. It would be very difficult, however, to draw a line between it and the need to pray in Hebrew. The resources Levi draws on stem from classical Italian culture, as the famous chapter on Dante's *Inferno* testifies. In the one short section in which he refers explicitly to prayer, it is with contempt, at least for the timing of this particular one. Schultz is swaying back and forth ecstatically, thanking God for having spared him in the latest selection for the gas chambers. If I were God, says Levi, I would spit on Schultz's prayer.[2] The larger canvas of the book, though, portrays human beings from whom everything is taken away—their name, their appearance, the slightest personal belonging, control over their bodily functions. That nakedness hit me hard. I was not sure that in such circumstances Dante would do. In many cases, of course, nothing would do. People were too brutalized. I concluded that one needed to store up, as if for a famine. Among the provisions was the ability to join other Jews in prayer.

The stage was set for attending a synagogue, although that took several more years. Given that my first teaching job made me extraordinarily anxious, Kees, my graduate school advisor, suggested I either take up meditation or start attending services. For reasons that elude me, probably deeply pathological, I have an enormous aversion to meditation. I chose the other option. For almost three years, I went to Shabbat services in a shul in Mountain View, near Palo Alto, even riding my bike over hill and dale on a weekday to take a class with the rabbi, Shelley Lewis. Every time we come to "modim anakhnu lakh" in the "Amidah," the silent section of the liturgy, I remember that this gentle human being made me love this prayer. In subsequent years, I have attended other synagogues, probably my longest spell at the shtiebl in Los Angeles whose rabbi was Shmuel Miller. I do not identify a particular prayer with him. I owe him too much for that. After many years' lapse, I have started again, in Philadelphia, grateful that I have enough knowledge to participate.

Prayer is a very intimate matter. In many respects, I cannot say that I have learned how to pray, and even if I did, how would one convey that? Occasionally, at Shmuel Miller's shul, I would see one of the big burly North African men go up to the ark after services were over, and pray silently. Shmuel's wife, Margolit, also once prayed with such fervor that I knew something incommunicable, except in the prayer itself, was going on. For me, it is enough that I can engage in the process. This does not at all mean that I will be able to recite the "Sh'ma" at the crucial moment. For that, I might have started too late.

I do not see the return, however partial, to Jewish practice and Jewish learning, as a rebellion against my parents. Rather, it is an attempt to retrieve the ground under their feet. For many years, a photograph follows me every-where I move. In it, my mother is seated on one side of her father, two of her

---

2    Primo Levi, *Survival in Auschwitz*, trans. Stuart Woolf (New York: Collier Books, 1961), 118.

sisters flanking him on the other side. It is 1933, the year she left for Paris. Everyone is very young, except my grandfather whose white beard betrays his age, despite the skull cap that completely covers his head. His black *kapote*, a Hasidic outer coat, contrasts with the modern garb of his daughters, the light short-sleeved dresses of my mother's sisters, the pretty suit that my mother is wearing. The worlds had not split, at least in this household. The coexistence might not have been peaceful, but one cannot separate those young women from the father in whose house they grew up. I can reconstruct that house as little as I can reconstruct my father's world, no matter how many stories my mother might tell, and, in this case, there were not many. I proceed on the unproven assumption that that world provides a more layered soil for the protection of the person than either Communist ideology or Western liberalism. It is not a matter of some objective ideology ready for the picking, but of the intention of the searcher on a lifelong quest to recover this protection. I am not alone. Other people have preceded and accompanied me, extracting the edible fruit hidden inside the disposable peel.

My maternal grandfather, and three of his daughters, my mother seated on his right, 1933.

If I rebel against anything in my return to Jewish knowledge, it is against the sense that one can invent oneself from scratch. At first self-invention was a simple matter. It required ignoring or hiding the history from which one came. It now has a technological twist. One sends away a sample to a company, which, for a fee, provides one's genetic ancestry. Is this not way of bypassing one's real heritage, the one communicated in a most intimate way? Our culture seems intent on rooting us in our biological makeup while at the same time assuring us that we are not determined by it, since genetic engineering can in the future transform us, while hormone treatment and surgery do some of that work in the present. It is a confusing time. It should not, however, be taken to be the great liberator from the past. It merely subjects us to the whims of the present. On the other hand, to say that we are our parents' offspring does not mean that we mechanically repeat what was given. What was given needs to be probed and turned over and over. First of all, it needs to be confronted, not as blind loyalty but as our own memory. We are our memory. It is false consciousness to think that we can escape it. To be oneself from the inside is to have one's own memory, and not someone else's and not one given by statistical probabilities about descendance. I cry against this externalization of who we are.

I see that things have become very serious. From a rather banal list about the languages overheard in my home, I have landed in a definition of the human as such, and in a defense of one's sense of reality from coinciding with a Silicon Valley marketing campaign. Very often, I wish I had a lighter touch. But not everything is given. It is already good that not everything is up for grabs.

# 4

# Mental Illness

By 1976, my mother was hearing voices whose every command she had to obey in order to stay alive. When I would ask her why she stayed out all day, afraid to come home, she would answer that that was what they ordered. Who were the they? The neighbors. Which neighbors? The answer was always vague. She indicated that they had a way of speaking directly into her head. She was not interested in convincing me. The only matter of any importance was to deflect the mortal danger. Her very kind elderly physician told me the several times I consulted with him that without her consent, nothing could be done. Finally, two years after the first appearance of the voices, my mother did something egregious enough to be admitted to a psychiatric ward, even without her consent. One of the medications she was given was Haldol. It did suppress the voices, but not only them. Except for a few monosyllabic answers to questions, she stopped speaking until she was taken off the drug. I think now that I should have investigated other treatments. But the internet, with its subversion of the authority of doctors, had not yet appeared on the scene. Even more of a factor, perhaps, was that the drugs she was taking made my life easier. She was no longer wandering the streets of LA all day, following the orders of her voices to stay out of her apartment. I do not blame myself about this. But it was not what one could call heroic devotion.

I also have no bones to pick with the psychiatric wards themselves. These utterly controlled environments, akin to prisons, nonetheless became sites of respite and hope against hope for someone witnessing the complete unraveling of another human being. It was a sense of hope mixed with a strong dose of dread. Everything was rigidly regulated—electronic entrances, enforced group activities. The control was understandable, given the volatility and unpredictability of the patients, but it was also, inescapably, highly unnatural, a kind of alternate and bleak universe. My mother mechanically handed over to me a lowly wooden napkin holder that she had varnished and decorated in the obligatory arts and crafts session. In one of these wards, the one in Beverly Hills, in addition to the medication, she was assigned a therapist, a clear attempt at personalizing her treatment. Unfortunately, she was completely incapable of analyzing herself in the terms required, quite independently of the language barrier, which was in itself not insignificant. After a month, she would always be released, strictly a medical insurance calculation, but also unintentionally wise, since these places always exuded arctic air, despite the warmth of this or that individual staff member.

What really sticks in my craw occurred outside the ward itself. Upon releasing her, her doctors prescribed follow-up visits with a psychiatrist to whose office in Beverly Hills I would take her at regular intervals. All that comes to mind now are the spatial arrangements. He would sit behind the desk of his office, dressed in his impeccable suit, a framed photograph of his elegant wife and beautiful children behind him. My mother would sit on the other side of the desk, stooped, a bit frightened. I sat somewhere to the side. Like a bank teller filling out a form, he would ask her the three required questions: Was she suicidal, did she feel bad about herself, was she depressed? My mother would answer no to all these questions, without further comment. Minutes later, we would be out of the door, but not before he had exchanged some pleasant banter with me. To her, he paid no further attention. My mother had a weak spot for doctors, especially if they were what she considered to be *przysto-jny*, handsome. A little playfulness could have lifted the heaviness of her day for a few minutes. Throughout the many visits we made to his office, it never occurred to that man, basking in well-being, to part from the three-question script in this or any other way.

Departing from the script can be done. I saw it with my own eyes. Not too many months before my mother died, quite a few years after these rote visits to the psychiatrist, I became convinced that it would bring her comfort to say a *vidui*, a ritual confession. As ludicrous as the idea appears now, at the time I thought it would bring her some solace. She had sought out a rabbi in the beginning of the LA troubles, pouring out her heart, seeking help against her enemies. I brought my friend Shmuel Miller, although it was not his idea, maybe because he understood before I did that these rituals do not function out of context. He came dressed in his usual long grey garb, looking the part of a traditional rabbi she might have known from her childhood. My mother's reaction was one of fright, as if I had brought a priest for the purpose of dispensing the extreme unction, and, I suppose, in a way I had. Her fearful reaction had not entered into my computations, and at first, things went from bad to worse. Shmuel asked her some questions, mainly about her responsibilities to the Jewish community. I had never heard a vidui before, and not since either, and so I assume this is the form it takes in the observant Jewish world. My mother remained perfectly silent. Shmuel, without losing a beat, switched to speaking to her in Yiddish about her accomplishments, stressing what a great thing it was that she had raised me, and how well I had turned out. A smile appeared on her face. I am not convinced that she was basking in her child-rearing techniques. At least equally likely as the source of that smile was the very peculiar Yiddish with which Shmuel had addressed her. Despite his many years of study as a grown man in a Lithuanian yeshivah in Israel, he spoke it with a comically French accent, outside the range of its many possible variations. At the end of the visit, my mother had not confessed, but its success was not to be measured by that. Shmuel had spoken to her about her life, in her language, evoking in her a long-buried sense of humor.

A second moment of what I can only call grace occurred in the last retirement home in which she lived. The cooking and cleaning staff were primarily women from El Salvador, who were working for minimum wage, if that. In the fall of 1993, I decided to pay one of them to make sure that my mother, who had just had an operation, was taking her medication at lunch time, and generally to look in on her occasionally in the course of the day. This specialized attention was outside the staff's normal course of duty, the women having little time to spare in their schedule. It was Eliza I had in mind, someone my mother liked. She was probably a dozen years older than I was but I thought of her as of another generation because she was already a grandmother. I caught her in the stairwell, as I was going to my mother's room, explained what was needed, awkwardly assuring her that I would pay. She agreed immediately, but refused the money. It was not a fear of receiving money under the table. Much went on under the table in that nonetheless decent institution. "We all have mothers," was all Eliza said. A couple of months later, as her disease progressed, my mother had to be moved to a full-time nursing facility. At Christmas time, wanting to give presents to Eliza, and also to Mikaela, and to another mannish young woman whose name I do not remember, I showed up again at the retirement home. They asked about her, but for them life had flowed past this event. I was surprised. Such acts of kindness as theirs meant eternal gratitude on my part. Yes, on my part, but it did not mean an eternal accountability system on theirs. The moment had passed.

Moments of grace are difficult to capture without turning into cheap sentiment, the following even more subject to this than the preceding one. In the time I spent in LA during the last year of her life, I visited my mother daily, with few exceptions. We had our ritual gestures of welcome, devoid of display, so devoid of display, in fact, that I do not even remember what they were so many years later, with one exception. It was the day my cousins Janey and Joanne came to the retirement home. Janey, the older of the two, brought her toddler. In a picture taken that day, my mother is holding Matty, her face completely contorted by medication, staring into the camera as if into the void. But moments afterward, that same face became suffused with affection when I joined the gathering, a bit late. My mother never faked her emotions. She lived *à fleur de peau*, as the French expression goes, exposed to all the inner elements. I do not pretend to know why at this moment that smile appeared. I carefully hoard it. Maybe the rabbi who included the priests' blessing in the liturgy—"May God show you his face, and smile upon you"[1]—had seen a similar smile thousands of years ago.

\*\*\*

The technical name given for my mother's condition was paranoid schizophrenia, an obvious fit. She lived in another reality, in which she had to do the bidding of her persecutors, leading her to actions in this reality—barricading herself in her room for several days in one instance, fearing to enter her room during daylight hours for months on end in another. The doctor had told me that since schizophrenia had manifested itself so late, in my mother's early sixties, when it usually announces itself much sooner, this was a form of senility. This latter diagnosis hit me the wrong way from the start. She had been paranoid ever since I could remember, making the hearing of voices the most acute version of what I had known since childhood. I have already mentioned all the neighbors who disliked her, forcing us to move again and again, to which were added the many bosses or co-workers who plotted against her, and for which reason, she often changed jobs. I learned early on that it was futile to try to dissuade her. Once, in LA, she was so convinced that the upstairs neighbors were up to no good, that when the first rumbles of the 1971 earthquake started, she jumped out of bed to get a broom with which to hit the ceiling in response. Only the

---

1   The original verses from which the priestly blessing is taken is Numbers 6:23-27.

subsequent rumbles made her realize that she was up against a force of nature. I did not often have such arguments on my side.

I do not pretend to understand what led my mother to punish herself so relentlessly for so long even if I have my theories, like everyone else. But I do know that in the process, there was collateral damage. One of the most egregious was Morris. It happened after my mother had already been hospitalized once, but in a period of relative calm. She was living in the first retirement hotel of the series, across the street from MacArthur Park, in an area at some remove from the Fairfax neighborhood, which she might have chosen for that very reason. Morris was a recent widower, in his late seventies, maybe even eighty, in any case, much older than she. He had moved in to the Grandview Hotel not long after she did. A courtship began, nearly wordless, since he was American and did not speak any of the requisite languages. She enjoyed his attention, the rides in the big car for short trips around LA, someone to sit with side by side. They decided to get married. I asked a rabbi friend to officiate. The details of the ceremony blur because that very same night my mother threw Morris out, barricaded herself in her room, convinced that he was cheating on her with someone else, and had to be taken to the hospital again. Morris appeared on my doorstep the next day, so forlorn, seeking to understand. After she came back from the hospital, they still spent some time together, but less frequently. She tried to take care of him when he got sick. Not long afterward, he was moved into a nursing home.

Strange to say, perhaps, until she began to hear voices, I never associated my mother's paranoia with mental illness. This is simply the way she was. I envied children whose parents were more rational. In one example of my desire to escape that my mother would remind me of throughout my childhood, I had run enthusiastically to the wrong set of waiting parents at the exit of the school. But if I envied some, I also knew others beside myself who received less than textbook parenting. In our Fairfax neighborhood, I had several school friends whose parents had lived through the Second World War, whose behavior or demeanor, while different from my mother's, seemed erratic in ways not unlike hers. Mrs. B., for instance, a large woman with a twisted face, had remained hidden in a hole in a countryside farm near Lwów (now Lviv) for several years. She spoke very little. The details of the difficulties she caused my friend are now overshadowed in my memory by the suicide of Mr. B., an Auschwitz survivor, a few days before his daughter's wedding. As to R. W.'s parents, I met them once in their home. Survivors of Auschwitz as well, they spoke to me in an unmistakable Hungarian accent, perfectly friendly but rigid in their dress and manners. R. ended up anorexic in a period when the condition was hardly known, and a couple of years later, her older brother committed suicide in a university chemistry lab. My mother, until she started counting her breaths to satisfy the number allotted by her voices, seemed on a continuum of normalcy. It was tough to live with her but it looked as if living with one's parents was tough next door as well.

Yet my mother did hear voices. She acted on them. She was a danger to herself when she did. She was mentally ill. Saying it makes me uncomfortable. It is not so much the stigma attached to it, but the hierarchy of merit that seems to coincide with it. To say that I had a mentally ill mother makes it seem as if I had won the million-dollar lottery in the category of suffering, propelling me to the front of the line of my generation's complaints about their mothers. It is a peculiar kind of contest, in which I admit participating. So, your mother was cold, controlling? She made critical remarks? That does not even come close to cutting it, I say to myself. To each his portion, I know, but not well enough. After all, can the others claim that their mother was mentally ill? I beat them hands down. On the other hand, or perhaps on the same hand still, I want to rescue my mother from the label. Her horrific fears and misrepresentations of others' motifs do not get at her sense of humor, her storytelling, her immediate being of who she was. In the days before the very bad period, when she laughed, it would come from deep inside, a most satisfying sound. What would I be, were it not for her many stories, strewn throughout these pages? I recall her hands, which I would always hold before going to sleep when I was small, and which I held when she was much older, noticing the changes in smell and texture.

I also want to protest against the erasure of all that is not merely neurological, not merely the derailment of an individual psyche, in the label "mental illness." On the city bus these days, I hear all sorts of telephone conversations. Overhearing would not really be the right word, given the high pitch at which they are conducted. Many of them echo my mother's complaints—a co-worker or boss who is playing a dirty trick on the person talking, a landlord who wants to evict. Many of the riders on the bus are working class at best, at the mercy of many others, deprived of freedom in the economic realm. My mother's paranoia was a magnified expression of a very widespread powerlessness. More than that, although the crematoria she went in search of in 1978 did not exist in Los Angeles, they had existed in Poland and Germany, from 1942 onward and, in some cases, even earlier. She invented neither the murder of most of her family in Poland and Lithuania, nor her own arrest with the same intent in mind. She did not invent the extreme isolation of aging immigrants like herself in the United States and elsewhere. Her illness is a judgment on this world, on its barbarity. This does not make her less mentally ill, nor is this intended as some sort of adjudication of responsibility. The world is responsible, she is not. She is responsible, the world is not. But one gets sick within a specific world, and not only within one's head.

I recently read something like that in a novel. A college student diagnoses the clinical depression of her lover as a condition emanating from neoliberalism. I rolled my eyes, as perhaps the author intended the reader to do, underscoring the intellectualism of the very young. There may be events close to home, placing concrete relationships in the center, without which even terms like neoliberalism mean nothing. Among these events is the extreme isolation of the elderly to which I alluded. A Polish acquaintance, when I told her that my mother had had a rough time in the United States, asked why I had not continued to live with her. Did I not feel remorse for leaving her alone like that? The acquaintance, having emigrated from Poland for economic reasons, felt that had she stayed, she would have been with her mother constantly. An American colleague, on the other hand, praised me for spending a year on leave in Los Angeles during my mother's last illness, as if it were an extraordinary thing to do. I recognize neither of these attitudes, not the remorse and not the praise. Nor do I recognize the kind of contempt with which some American friends speak of their parents. They list their parents' hurtful ways, not only as accusations but also as if their parents were people they could size up from the safe distance of their own impeccable morality. I cannot untangle my own relationship to my mother. I will not be buried near her, for the same reason that I chose not to live with her as an adult. But whenever I am in Los Angeles for more than a few days, I visit her grave. Once, I brought my very good friend Pien to the cemetery with me. She was herself already failing, in her late eighties. We sat on the grass next to the tombstone. "You did not even like your mother very much," she said, à propos of who knows what. It had not occurred to me that one could like or dislike one's parents. My admiration for the honesty is mitigated by my shudder at the objectivity. I did not want my mother to hear Pien's remark.

\*\*\*

I had mentioned that my mother often told the story of the Vel D'hiv. In mid-July 1942, the French police came to her door, and took her away to a large sports stadium, the above mentioned Vélodrome d'hiver, where she joined thousands of other foreign-born Jews, over thirteen thousand to be more precise, most of them women and children and old men. The conditions were extreme—great heat in the sealed space, no toilet facilities, no food or water, and very little medical personnel. The overwhelming majority of those arrested and kept there were in short order sent to concentration camps and then to Auschwitz, with almost no survivors. I had heard my mother's story about it so often that even today I do not fully grasp how exceptional her own behavior was. In that terrorized group of people, in which trying to escape meant immediate death by shooting, she took the stairs and walked out.

My mother's story was exceptional in another way. She told it as a great moral drama, in which the judgments were buried in the actions themselves, my very own biblical tale. Two French police officers had come to her door early one morning. She did not open the door. They announced loudly that they would be back in two hours. My mother understood this to mean that they were giving her time to escape. A journalist friend who had been hiding in my parents' apartment in fact took this opportunity to flee. My mother did not. As she told it, she felt too weak to move, having just returned the day before from a hospital stay for an appendicitis operation. She was also disoriented and demoralized. My father was already in the transit camp in Compiègne, having been arrested months earlier. She was alone. The French police came back, and, at the beginning the same scenario repeated itself. They knocked. She did not open the door. Then she heard the voice of the concierge. She is in there, he assured them, I did not see her leave. Under threat, my mother opened the door. She asked the two officers to be taken on a stretcher, and took nothing with her, just draping a light coat over what she was wearing.

The chaos in the Vel D'hiv produced an unexpected effect. It galvanized her. Thinking that her coat resembled a nurse's cape, a Florence Nightingale style she said had been popular that year, she asked one of the few medical attendants if she could take her hat. "Je ne peux pas, Madame," the woman answered. My mother then decided to take her chances anyway, hoping the coat would be enough to pass as a nurse or medical assistant. She found an exit and started walking down the stairs. Once outside, she walked into the bistro across the street. A woman from Marseilles was tending the bar. No, she could not hide my mother, she answered to my mother's query. It was too dangerous because the "Boches" (the French pejorative for the Germans) were frequent patrons of her establishment. But seeing how weak my mother looked, she gave her money for the metro and walked with her, supporting her by the arm until they got there. When my mother reached her apartment, the concierge was surprised to see her, having already sealed the door. She told him that there had been a mistake in her case, quickly took some things and then went to a clandestine Jewish organization that fabricated false papers. She first used those papers to work as a Polish nanny for a Swedish couple in Paris, later leaving Paris to join an older sister and her young son who were hiding in the countryside of Corrèze, in the Free Zone.

I retell this story now not because there is any direct line to draw between it and her subsequent schizophrenia. To say, as I did, that her illness reflected the world she had lived in is not to attribute causes. The many balls that constitute a life all bounce in the air at the same time. But the roundup of the Vel D'hiv remains nonetheless relevant to the story I have just told because people's response to a marked person was at the heart of my mother's tale, as it is in mine about her illness. Her account cast no blame either on the two French policemen or on the nurse in the Vel D'hiv. The police indirectly tried to help her, and the nurse did not betray her, seemingly sorry that she could not do what my mother asked. The concierge was another type altogether. Nothing obligated his betrayal of my mother. His life was not at stake. No one had asked him to say a thing. But he went that extra step, exposing another person to destitution and possible death. Did he pronounce the words he did because he confused conformity to the powers that be with morality? Was it venality that made him seal the apartment so soon? My mother's judgment was implacable, made even more so because it was implicit. Her gratitude to the woman from Marseilles was equally unwavering. She had gone that extra step in the other direction. One is reminded of a poem that that irreverent French singer, Georges Brassens, put to music, in which all those who have given a piece of bread, a bit of heat, a helping hand to the one in need will be transported across the heavens.[2]

Whenever I heard the story in my youth, I always hoped that I would be able to say "Oui, Madame." Here is my hat. Here is my home. I was hoping against hope that I would be able to overcome my great timidity, my unwillingness to stand out, for which my mother berated me all my life. I think now, if one responds kindly "Non, Madame," and looks the other way when someone makes a move to escape, and—much, much better—if one can say "Non, Madame," and then take someone under the arm to the metro, that is already a very great thing. Should one aspire to more than that? The world would collapse if more were not possible. At the crucial moment, I still pray that I would be able to say "Oui, Madame." But, like my mother, I have come to see small

---

2    I am referring to "Chanson pour l'Auvergnat," also known as "Elle est à toi, cette chanson."

instances of excess, in either direction, as the common currency, as what ordinary people can refuse to do, or can agree to do.

There was an indefinable quality to my mother's story about the Vel D'hiv. She related all events in a detached tone of voice. I have heard this tone in other accounts from the war, as if to introduce any emotion were to cloud over the facts. It is as if my mother had read all that has been written on how to represent abnormality when it seeps into daily life and becomes normal. Although it is not a comparable event, mental illness, both for the person suffering from it, and for those around it, is a permanent abnormality irrupting into the normal and grotesquely merging with it. As horrifying as my mother's voices were, they became part of my daily life, a routine aspect I had to tend to, as routine as calling her every evening around six to make sure she had made it home from her wanderings on the street. A recurrent dream I had during this period of her illness was the most salient sign that not all was routine. I remember little of its details after so many years, except that I would suddenly come stark awake, seeing my mother crucified and being eaten to shreds by animals. But this was in my dreams. In the daytime, her illness was simply something I had to attend to, mostly through a phone call or a visit.

My other reaction surprises me by its naivete. After all, I was already twenty-four when my mother first started hearing voices. I thought we were being singled out, that normal lives do not include such pain. I know now that most people encounter some completely undigestible sorrow, and that my mother's condition was exceptional only in its form. But no matter how much I know about abnormal normalcy, I cannot tell the story of her illness in that tone of detachment in which she told the story of the Vel d'hiv. I become once again the child who wishes it were not so.

# 5

# Money

## Renting

Some people remember old phone numbers. I remember rents:

$80.00—our apartment in New Jersey
$120—our first apartment in Los Angeles
$160—my last apartment in Los Angeles
$450—my apartment in Menlo Park
$300—my first apartment in Lancaster, PA

Some of these amounts mean something in isolation, and some mean something in relationship to each other, as is the case for the first two. When my mother and I arrived in LA in the summer of 1968, the Greyhound bus let us off in the downtown area. I looked with consternation at the rundown buildings, simultaneously relieved that we could afford to live in one of them. My mother, paying no heed to my remarks to this effect, headed straight to the Jewish neighborhood of the city, commonly known as Fairfax, after its main commercial street. The building we lived in for the next two years was fairly new, but so cheaply built that it already looked past its prime. We lived on the second of its two floors, in one of its approximately ten units, whose entrances all faced sideways rather than the street. The part of the building facing the street had a few parking spaces underneath the second floor. The rent, by my reckoning, was not modest at all. At a whopping $120, it was a full $40 more than what we had paid in New Jersey. I was seized by terror and admiration for my mother's ways. After all, it was very unlikely that sewing collars, linings and button holes would prove to be more lucrative in the factories of LA than it had been back in New Jersey. How would we live?

The problem was quickly solved. Shortly after moving in, we took a stroll down Fairfax Avenue, dotted with many small businesses, among which seven Jewish bakeries within two blocks. We entered one of them, Fairfax Bakery, the smallest and oldest of them all. The owner, a kind Hungarian Jewish woman, had thought she was hiring my mother when affirming that indeed a job was available. My mother pointed to me. After some hesitation, given that all the other sales women ranged from their mid-forties to sixty, and I was merely sixteen, she decided to take her chance. In less than five minutes, I had joined the American work force. For three years, I sold danish, kichel, strudel and babkas; water bagels, egg bagels, kaiser rolls and bialys; rye, pumpernickel and corn bread, small or large, thin-sliced or thick-sliced, to all and sundry: the many Eastern European immigrants in the area, the bikers, the hippies who frequented the Free Press bookstore across the street, the occasional Scientologists, the very occasional Groucho Marx. Those twenty hours a week kept us rolling in baked goods. But, more importantly, the salary made up the difference between the New Jersey and the LA rent.

It is strange to think that those twenty hours did not cramp my time. I still had two years of high school to go, a period I recall as very unpleasant. But none of my widely shared adolescent angst had anything to do with time constraints. Most of my friends had part-time jobs, with hours equivalent to mine. We complained about everything under the sun. Breaking up our day into hourly units, into which all our activities would appear as homogenous blocks on a calendar, would not have occurred to any of us. In exchange for a loosely scheduled life, most of us did not get the current enrichments of body and soul—the athletic activities, the art lessons, the community service—in which so many contemporary middle-class high school and college-age students engage. It will surprise no one to hear that participating in the life of the bakery had its own rewards. It was a stage, in which, dressed in my white uniform, I would act my part, observing the interactions of my co-workers, imitating their way with the customers, learning to place the baked goods just so in their display cases, very occasionally, toward the end, even opening and closing the store by myself. The sounds of Yiddish, the interactions with the young men who ran the bookstore, to which I would often repair on my break, the teasing and flirting with the owners' huge sons—this was good. I enjoyed it then, and wish I had taken notes because that entire world has disappeared—the Jews, the hippies, the bikers, Groucho Marx, but maybe not the Scientologists.

The other rents that belong together on my list are the last LA one—at $160—and the first Lancaster one—at $300. They stand out for being unusually good deals. In neither case was my business acumen involved in the slightest. My last LA apartment, a small house, in fact, came to me by way of my friend Sharon's parents, who lived next door, and who alerted me to the vacancy. As to my first Lancaster rent, it was not at first particularly low, only becoming so in the course of the next eleven years. The landlords, an old Lancaster county couple who owned many properties in the area, preferred stability over increased revenue, especially since as they aged, they did only the minimum to maintain the property. My arrangements with both the LA and the Lancaster landlords were, of course, business ones. But they were also face-to-face relations. We chatted regularly. I came to know something of their life stories, of the city at an earlier point of its history, of the interior of their own apartments or houses. The owner of the LA house would come over frequently to work in the garden in the back. One day, as I was watching him tend the fig trees, he interrupted his activity to hand me his dentures. They were new, and worthy of my admiration, or so he thought. It is true that he was already failing somewhat, prone to repeating the story of his divorce. His wife had walked out in the middle of vacuuming.

By contrast, the Menlo Park rent, at $450 a month, filled me with indignation. A converted garage with aubergine-colored walls, as my landlady insisted on calling them, it was one third the size of my LA house and cost nearly three times as much. Silicon Valley was still a few years down the road but this place of perfect weather not far from San Francisco had been a wealthy enclave for a long time already. Despite its past as a garage, the apartment was lovely, with a small alcove into which to place a bed, and a fenced-in yard with some pine trees. But that amount still rankled. In the complicated calculus of what I was willing to spend much money on, rents were not included until very recently when, near retirement, I began to contemplate the brevity of existence. In this, I have been assisted by the financial advisor, who remarked, when I was fearful about the possibility of paying at least two thousand dollars for a one-bedroom apartment if I moved to Philadelphia, that I should not worry about it because I was not going to live that long anyway.

Since all these amounts have lodged themselves in my memory without any concerted effort on my part, I suspect they reveal the depth of my identity as a renter. In the American context, this is a puzzling maladaptation. Even when I could have afforded to buy, I remained unmoved by all talk of equity, nest egg, investment, not to mention reverse mortgages. I have always equated my disinterest with a form of moral purity, vaguely aware that it was mixed with less noble sentiments. Even very recently, when I tried to break my pact with renting, a betrayal which lasted less than two weeks, I nearly kissed the building contractor who dissuaded me from buying a house, despite the fact that its structure was sound. Around the same time, when a friend, to help me decide, asked whether I was ready to assume the responsibilities of house ownership, I responded with a "No" that sounded nothing so much as a sigh of relief.

I date to a conversation with a younger colleague the beginning of my awareness that buying a house bestowed the seal of responsibility, a little like a bar mitzvah. Already in my fifties at the time, I was curious as to why he was buying a house at such a young age, even before he had received tenure. As long as he was renting, he said, he did not feel like an adult. I was stunned. Like an expression that one hears for the first time, and then hears again and again in subsequent days, the inexorable link between house buying and maturity began to appear everywhere. Most recently I caught it again in my friend Alan's delight at his son's purchase of his first home. He was so proud, he said, that his son was exhibiting responsibility in a new arena. While I still do not grasp the full moral gravity of house ownership, I do understand that what I had always aligned with moral purity—renting—is, in the larger view, morally suspect behavior. I would like to get to the bottom of this. It must be that I suppress the real reason for my reticence: fear of debt, fear of electricians and plumbers, fear of the grave, fear of gardening, fear of entering the mainstream of the human race. The latter might be the most damning. It translates into the refusal of the staid expectations of middle-class life. My father had fought in the Spanish Civil War. My mother had married him. Can one buy a house after such a heroic past? Not for me the lowly preoccupations of mere mortals.

But one must be fair, even to oneself. If, undeniably, fear has played a role in my insistence upon renting, it may not be the only factor or even the determining factor. I have been afraid of other things, and in at least some cases, have overcome my fear. One also has to consider that between 1950 and 1970, approximating the first twenty years of my life, everyone rented, a norm to which I have clung, as if parting with it would erase my past. Looking back, of course, I notice that not everyone rented. My mother's friends in Brussels— Madame Pinczewski and Madame Urbach—owned their homes, as did my classmate Danielle Vermeylen, whom I would pick up on my walk to the Arthur Diderich elementary school. She would come out of a house, not an apartment building. But if I never noticed, it might have been because no talk of buying and selling homes or apartments ever entered into any conversation that I can remember until much, much later in my life. On 51st Street, in New Jersey, the whole block teemed with tenants—from the Cuban immigrants in the large apartment house on the corner, to the mostly Jewish immigrants in the five-story apartment houses in the middle of the street, to the more well-to-do denizens in the stately apartment building on the other corner, facing the Manhattan skyline—all renters. It is true that three years into our sojourn in Weehawken, my cousins of 17, 51st street moved to a house in the suburbs in another county. It had a front lawn and a back yard, maybe even a white picket fence. They acquired a mutt called Stanley. I was unaware at the time that they were living the American dream, merely sorry that they had moved so far away. Renting remained what everyone did, even if everyone didn't.

But here, matters become complicated. Surely, I have not been attached to all aspects of my past. If I were to wager why I remained attached to this one, it is because it was intertwined with a moral code. There was virtue in living with few things, with what was necessary. It was a virtue that did not promote itself as such. People did not pat themselves on the back. It was embedded in the way people lived or, more precisely, as times changed, I saw the hidden virtue of what was largely an unchosen way of life. It was not ascetic, but there was some sense of limit which did not feel restrictive. My mother's clothes, for instance, were well tailored, and of good quality during the years in question, but she had few of them. Similarly, my favorite dress, a red-checkered woolen affair, with a green stripe down the middle, was of good quality. I wore it to school happily every day until Mrs. Berger who lived two floors below us opened the door as I was sauntering down the stairs expressly to let me know that American children do not wear the same outfit day in and day out. In Brussels, we had worn uniforms, sparing parents the cost of a wardrobe.

My favorite dress, New Jersey, 1963.

Other aspects of our life in Europe seem even more like a lost continent than our sartorial habits. We did not have a refrigerator. My mother, like everyone else, shopped for food almost every day. In rare instances, in cooler weather, when perishables were left over, we put them on the window sill at night. We also did not have a bathtub in some of the apartments in which we lived, taking baths in a basin once a week, supplementing this regularly with a visit to the public baths. It was perfectly natural to live this way, not a privation. The privation was not to have a steady income with which to cover the basic expenses. In the years of my father's unemployment and debts left in the aftermath of his death in Brussels, the only reason we did not experience privation directly was that friends of my parents helped. Once in the United States, our income stabilized even if it remained low. My memory was that it was enough, not because my mother and I had individually decided that it was but simply because it was self-evidently so. The underside of this acceptance of limits was the moral condemnation of a society which allows destitution. Not to have a roof over one's head, not to have enough to eat, this was crossing a line into "not enough." It was worth a revolution to redress it. To this day, it remains the only political issue that engages me viscerally.

We are told that the 1970s marked the onset of consumer culture. This has turned the hidden pact with limits into an idiosyncrasy, of which I am a prime example. For a long time, I refused to own a car. After all, there were buses. Only when I moved to a city with a very sparse public transportation system did I relent, buying a new car because it would require less attention than a used one, although I refused power steering and air conditioning. When I was offered a desk top computer for my office, I asked for an electric typewriter instead, until it became clear I could not function at my college on this nonetheless quite practical device. For a long time, I owned very few books, even though they were the tools of my profession, preferring to borrow them from the library. One has to be able to move quickly, if circumstances demanded it. As the decades accumulated, I also began to accumulate books, recognizing that the circumstances had not demanded it. More recently, I have refused smart phones and GPS devices as dangerous frills, frills because we do not need them, and dangerous because they track us. If I could have refused an electronic key to my latest car, I surely would have. There was still a lock on the driver's door. What's wrong with a manual key? These latest refusals, I realize make me faintly ridiculous, a cartoon figure like Mr. Magoo, tooting about, blind to the century I am living in. I accept the humor at my expense, and try to participate in creating it.

The hidden pact with limits that I grew up with contained a not so faint, diffuse contempt of wealth, coexisting with a lusty appreciation for some of the pleasures it can bring. The rich will always be among us, and one graciously bends to this fact. But especially if one was an academic, even if one did not turn one's nose up at a pleasure that came one's way, one did not actively strive to achieve wealth. Recently, when I discovered that a colleague, beyond owning his own home, had bought several properties as investments, I was surprised. It is as if he had violated Pascal's three orders. In the order of the mind, to which intellectuals belong, one recognizes as great only intellectual achievement. We have no business seeking greatness through the accumulation of material goods, betraying who we claim to be. As to Pascal's highest order, the order of the heart, like a true member of the order of the mind, I see the greatness of pursuing humility and charity, but the practice of these virtues often pales in comparison to a really well thought out idea about them. Unfortunately.

I am tempted to call this peculiar harking back to the moral code of my youth unworldliness but it does not fit very well. In the first place, unworldliness requires the background of a religious tradition, in which a good beyond the pleasures of this world—let us call it service to God or to the Revolution— is of paramount importance, given shape through communal practices and teachings. Since that common background has faded, my refusal to acquire the ordinary tools of our world increasingly becomes a form of assertion, a way of standing out, rather than a cultivation of a good not defined by the ownership of those objects. Secondly, it would be a misnomer to characterize my parents, from whom my moral universe cannot help but derive, as unworldly. How could they have been if the very first objects upon which my eyes alighted was their Louis XV-style furniture? My father, in everyone's stories, was the very image of prodigality, spending money on all and sundry. To be sure, this is an unattachment to wealth, but one must have it in order to exhibit this virtue. My mother, from a different class and temperament, was not prodigal. But much of her frugality was forced upon her by circumstances. She had a healthy appetite for the pleasures of this world.

I still recall, for instance, finding ourselves in a pretty little restaurant, at a table with red checkered table cloths, after one of our moves to a yet humbler dwelling. These infrequent indulgences made me nervous but they were also thrilling. Limits had limits. Who knew one could taste something beyond them, break out if only for a short period? In the same spirit, even after my father's death, my mother insisted that we take short vacations, paltry affairs compared to the lengthier ones in the days of better fortune. The bus would take us to various sites in California, Lake Elsinore, for instance. We did not quite know what to do once we got here, but we were on vacation. Occasionally, my mother's thumbing of her nose at necessity would manifest itself in a purchase. This is how a coffee table completely made of mirrors wended its way into our living room in Los Angeles, reflecting from several angles all the rest of the humdrum furniture we owned. She had found it on sale in a higher end design store, its fancifulness pleasing her. Much later, she bought a set of very delicately painted Polish china, a dinner set for eight. She had not been receiving guests for a very long time already, and, as it turned out, moved into a retirement home very soon thereafter. It too had been on sale, but completely unnecessary, except perhaps for its beauty. It may be that she bought it with me in mind, even though to that point I had given not the slightest indication that I would ever have a household that would require such formal dinnerware.

Even if the category of unworldliness, understood as disdain of material pleasures, does not fit my parents, it remains true that for neither was the pursuit of wealth or even comfort a concerted goal. Something else, not clearly defined, was always more important, the distant remnant, perhaps, of a tradition, in which money, although not disdained, was not the highest good. "Torah is the best merchandise," the rabbis tell us, indicating that its study, pursued for its own sake, *lishma*, gives the greatest reward. Neither of my parents studied Torah, of course. But something of that sense of lishma, or *le shem shamaym*, for the sake of heaven, was transferred to the intellectual life, to the arts, to my father's quixotic pursuit of the Revolution, to friendships. These were not hobbies, but life itself.

Among my mother's stories was the one in which she managed to put aside enough money so that when my father came back from the concentration camp, they could take a vacation. She had worked as a nanny under false papers for part of the war, spending much of the rest of it in hiding, neither of which particularly conducive to accumulating savings. My father returned one fine evening, finding her even though she had rented a room far from the apartment in which they had lived together. She had been reading when she heard a knock at the door. There he stood, so alarmingly thin. They had not seen each other for at least three years. And off they did go on vacation. It could not have been much later because my father is still very thin in the two photographs that remain. In one they are both in bathing suits, my mother's very ill fitting, since she had made it herself. In the second, they are sitting among their friends, some of whom I came to know, all still young, all having recently returned either from hiding or from German slave labor or death camps. All that is good in the world is captured in those photographs—love and friendship. One needed little else, just enough money to be able to celebrate those good things.

My parents on vacation just after the war.

My own approach to money resembles that of my parents. With all my resistance to unnecessary frills, I do not spurn the goods of this world. My apartment is spacious, in a good neighborhood. I occasionally buy not inexpensive clothes for the sheer pleasure of it. Traveling brings me joy. But there is an invisible line whose presence I sense when I cross it, beyond which lies indecency. Let some people pursue wealth. It is the order they are in. But it cannot be the only order, or the most respected order. I do not mean to suggest that we can live without any concern for money. As much of the above shows, I was and am concerned about it, like everyone else. But, as everyone also knows, life is about a desire neither shaped nor filtered by money. Am I exaggerating to suggest that we are no longer able to articulate such a desire? In response to the challenge, I would like to paint a portrait. It does not belong to the gallery of family photographs. But something of my family history has led me to it. I do not pretend it was a straight line.

## My friend Shmuel

I came to know Shmuel because he had an interest in the French Jewish philosopher Emmanuel Levinas, under whom he had studied briefly in Poitiers.

Having heard that I had translated some of his work, he had asked a mutual acquaintance to introduce us. I remember that first face-to-face conversation in the bare living room of those days. We sat drinking coffee, he in his knee-length kapote, I in my jeans. We talked animatedly. It was the beginning of a long friendship, an intellectual friendship, one might say, but that covers a very large territory, in both our cases.

Shmuel, his wife, and what came to be five children lived simply, as evidenced in that nearly unfurnished front room. There was never much money since he made his living as a *sofer*, a Torah scribe, refusing to take any payment for his service as a rabbi of his small congregation, whose members met in a converted garage at the back of his house. The simplicity was not merely the result of an unstable income. He had refused the additional salary that supervising *kashrut* might have brought him, knowing from personal experience how corrupt the world of certifying kosher meat could be. His was a one-man stand against accumulation, based on a notion of *bitahon*, trust, reliance on a source not of this world. He would speak to me of the halakhic injunction against the taking of interest. He had the bars taken from the windows of their house, claiming that the best defense against theft was the continual traffic of people to and from the house, which indeed was heavy.

Shmuel's unworldliness—his unconcern with wealth or fame as ends in themselves—did not imply an ignorance of the ways of the world. On the contrary, he closely followed the politics of several different countries, listening to and reading all sorts of venues in several languages. Well informed in a variety of subject matters, he surprised me occasionally by having gotten to an academic source much earlier than I had, and was surprised in turn when I did not know some important figure in French intellectual life. In Los Angeles, he was renowned for his mastery of Jewish sources, and frequently consulted as a legal expert. His reputation was such that in the few times that we went to the Pico-Robertson area, which had a large observant Jewish population, people from North Africa would greet him by kissing his hand, a gesture which he tried to avoid but could not always. He cooked well, took pleasure in beautifying the garage/synagogue, which became a place filled with light, with wooden bookshelves against the walls, lined with carefully bound traditional Jewish texts, *sefarim*. Blue tiles surrounded the wooden ark, and oil lamps hung from the ceiling, in the style of Tunisian synagogues. Those who prayed there looked out into a garden, nicely landscaped, with several fig trees. He also sang well, and was keenly aware of the musical traditions of the Middle Eastern world, both Jewish and non-Jewish.

His knowledge of the world included his many travels. Before he came to Los Angeles, his field work in anthropology, preceding his rabbinic studies, had taken him to sub-Saharan Africa. His political involvement in '68 France had brought him to Albania. Religious learning took him to Jerusalem, where he spent eight years studying at a Lithuanian yeshiva. In the time that I knew him, his interest in a non-Westernized Jewish life frequently took him to Djerba, in Tunisia, where he briefly contemplated resettling. Some unresolved issues among Muslims and Jews in Yemen brought him there, his Arabic sufficient to communicate without difficulty. It was one of his last major trips, and his enthusiasm was great. It was another life, something that had escaped the net of globalization. He spoke with excitement of the ceremonial swords men still wore, seeing in them a defense of an integrity whose very sense had disappeared elsewhere. As the Arabic he used in Yemen indicates, Shmuel spoke several languages, his native French, of course, but also Hebrew, which was the language he spoke with his children in the early years. Surprisingly, or perhaps not, since it is the daily language of that community, in the Lithuanian yeshiva in Jerusalem he had learned Yiddish. With the exception of the latter, all of these languages found their way into his English, whose intonation remained solidly French. Understanding his Torah interpretations, delivered in this mix, required acrobatic flights over lexical boundaries. I was always very proud that I followed him.

Notwithstanding his own refusal to pursue wealth, he was on good terms with many of the wealthy Jews of the city, especially those from the Sephardic or Mizrahi communities. Until his position on Israel made him into a persona non grata, he would often solicit donations from one or the other of them—for the young brides too poor to purchase wedding dresses, for the Yemeni Jews still left in Yemen. He himself had come from a well-to-do family, as far as I could tell. His father had been a highly placed military officer in the French army, originally from Algiers, where he himself was born. His parents had a vacation home in Spain. But whatever his family circumstances, he seems to have forged a code of his own. He would not have put it this way. As far as he was concerned, he was living the Jewish tradition as a separation from the world, as a protest. A protest against what exactly? He might have said against the loss of a sense of life as a service to God. He did not use that word much, but he also did not avoid it.

I am very wary of references to God, the result of having grown up in a world in which the word conjures a narrow, stifling way of thought and life. Whatever it was that Shmuel was serving, it seemed to be the opposite, breaking out of conventional understandings and group solidarity as an end in itself again and again. It was as if he saw something the existence of which was confirmed by his behavior, his willingness to risk his vital interests. When in the Jewish world most others ignored the plight of the Palestinians or were fervent supporters of the state, he spoke out, writing a powerful short essay about the responsibility of the observant community for Baruch Goldstein's murder of Palestinians at prayer in Hebron. Most Jews were horrified by the murders, but if they did put the blame on the Orthodox community, they were usually not a part of it. He was. The beginning of that essay reveals the personal burden he assumed. "Baruch, my brother," he began. In another instance, dressed in his long black coat, he testified against a Jewish developer who was dispossessing Palestinians in East Jerusalem, only to be spat upon by a fellow Jew who called him a traitor. In at least the last decade that I knew him, he went further, denying the possibility of being faithful to Jewish ways and having a sovereign state at the same time, sympathizing with the Neturei Karta, a subsect of the Satmar Hasidim, whose willingness to live in utter poverty in order not to take money from the State of Israel he admired. In the last years of his life, he exhibited enormous sympathy for Sufi practices and for traditional Islamic ways of life, basing his interest on the work of the son of Maimonides, who himself imported Sufi terminology in his interpretation of Jewish biblical texts. I remember that I myself recoiled when he suggested that prostration should become a more frequent practice in Jewish liturgy. Toward the end of his life, he was exploring bridges between traditional practitioners, independent of their group affiliation, so far did he think the contemporary Jewish people had departed from its mission.

His end, at once slow and rapid, was heartbreaking. He and his wife divorced, which shook him to the core. That first year, after his wife left, he had to have nearly all his teeth pulled out, but refused to have temporary implants of any kind. It was partially financial but not altogether. I had offered to help with the costs, as others must have, to no avail. It was as if he were doing penance, humbling himself for the wrongs he had committed. Maybe those bare gums were also a visible way of expressing his loss. One could live without many things but he was not yet used to living without her. Still, after the initial shock, life and color returned to the house. The bare living room filled with low couches in colorful fabrics, in the Moroccan style. He enjoyed becoming the father he could not be when his wife took care of most practical tasks involving their welfare. With a scholar from Florida, he began translating the writings of Rabbi David ben Maimon, along with providing a commentary. He dreamt of getting funds to research some ancient Jewish manuscripts in Aleppo. On at least one day of the week, the house was filled with musicians of Middle Eastern music. At his Shabbat table, one could still find people from many walks of life, and from different corners of the world.

Yet something began to unravel, at the center of which was his health. The medicine he had taken for years to abate the pain of his severe arthritis caused side effects, eventually compromising his kidneys and stomach. He became prone to all sorts of other conditions, suffering from several bouts of pneumonia, frequently losing his balance, feeling a generalized weakness. It made his always precarious economic circumstances yet more so. The other problem eating away at his livelihood, of course, was his growing distance from the Jewish community on which his daily bread depended. After all, a sofer works exclusively among practicing Jews, whatever their level of practice. They are the ones who need a new Torah scroll. His isolation became such that the *baalei batim*, the powerful leaders of the community to whom he could previously appeal for one or another project of his, did not return his calls.

In the last two years of his life, whenever I came to LA, I would often meet him in a coffee shop not far from his house. He loved to sit there and sip a creamy chocolate drink, his clothes now crumpled. We would engage in the same lively conversations as always, after which I would drive him home. Watching him get out of the car, and make his way haltingly, was to watch a homeless man, despite the fact he was clearly heading toward his front door. Once, when I was in town, I took him to a doctor. In the waiting room, he refused to give the phone numbers of people to contact in case of an emergency, writing in a bunch of arbitrary numbers instead. "Shmuel," I reproached him, "you have children." "I am alone," he said. It may have been an overly dramatic gesture, but I do not think he was reproaching his children. He was alone, despite them.

One day, he had a massive stroke. When I heard the news of his death, like everyone close to him, I could not stop crying. Not in LA at the time of his memorial service, I heard that his sons simply broke down, reproaching themselves in front of their community for having failed him. I too felt what I imagine was their love, and their sorrow at having failed him. He had asked me at various points to respond publicly to some French Jewish intellectuals who were, he claimed, taking an ideological stance against Islam in their attack on a French Muslim intellectual. I still have the letter to the editor that I wrote to *Le Monde*, but never sent, not feeling sufficiently part of the contemporary French political and intellectual landscape to engage in a debate. A long time before any talk of boycott, he had reproached me for traveling to Israel for conferences. It was collaboration to go and pretend that nothing was wrong, he said. When I told him that even though he was right, I could not bring myself to cut off my ties in the way he suggested, he accepted it, but not without saying that my unwillingness to speak and act would cost everyone in the end.

Most harsh about his end is that he himself may have lost sight of that reality that shone through his behavior. In one of the last images I have of him, he is lying in bed, unable to get out much because the latest series of strokes or perhaps some other condition made it very difficult for him to keep his balance. He had already fallen heavily a couple of times, unable to lift himself up without help. He did have some help. His former wife would show up after work every day to take care of him. The children who remained at home were very attentive, especially his second oldest son, who devoted himself particularly to his care. A couple of friends would stay the night when no one else was available. When I came to visit, I would find him quiet, staring out the window, a computer near at hand, but often unused. What was he seeing? There were some beautiful trees on that side, allowing in a lovely subdued light, despite the tall wall of the neighboring house. His quiet was impenetrable.

Shmuel remains my teacher. I take from his life the reality of something beyond this world, devotion to which is what makes us human, and not merely sophisticated animals. I also take from his life a parable about financial security. Shmuel worked very hard, and had a business side, as strange as this might sound. But he was unwilling to plan for the future, for sickness and old age. His solution turned out to be dying when he could no longer support himself. But dying may not happen on schedule. A modicum of financial stability seems essential. If one refuses, however, to bow to the majority's view, either on their practice of kashrut certification or the Israeli-Palestinian conflict, how can one guarantee a minimal financial stability? And, if one does not have a minimum to live on, this can lead to the breaking of the very moral backbone that had led to the isolation in the first place. The most painful part of this story to me is that even a great man cannot square that circle.

I have gone back to visit Shmuel's children several times since his death. They have a touching loyalty to him, receiving me royally in memory of him, asking me to tell them what we used to argue about, whether I have any of his writings. In the hallway leading to the synagogue, a photograph of him wearing his phylacteries is pinned to the wall. Their seriousness about Jewish learning is most touching of all. The youngest son, who has taken over the running of the synagogue, like his father, takes no money for it, engaging in a separate business as his livelihood. His daughter, who works all day in real estate company, teaches Torah classes to women. Everyone is always engaged in some halakhic discussion at some point during a meal. Gone, however, is a certain flavor, the flavor of Shmuel's particular unworldliness. One of his sons wanted to know when I visited what I meant when I said that Shmuel had a vision of being Jewish as a protest against the ways of the world. I try. It is no doubt very good that they have not caught the bug of unworldliness, in Shmuel's style. What makes it that I miss it so?

## Topsy turvy

A Polish acquaintance who had studied English for some months in Great Britain became close to one of her professors. She took the opportunity of one of his visits to her country to invite him to her parents' house for dinner. He is a strict vegetarian, she told them, warning them against preparing any meat dishes. The evening of the dinner there were indeed many vegetable dishes, but her father had also insisted on having one meat dish on the table, and not because he wanted to eat it. To have served only vegetables, he told her, did not sufficiently do honor to the guest.

This behavior is neither worldly nor unworldly. It is irrational, at least if looking through the lens of modern economic theory. Yes, serving meat is a sign of one's willingness to put oneself out financially in order to show respect. But why do so when you have been expressly told the guest will not recognize this as a sign of respect but might see it as the very opposite? Irrationality, however, is too vague a term for the strangeness of our behavior around money. Examples abound in which money, what is measurable par excellence, turns into the symbol of what cannot be measured. For instance, in our possession after my father's death were two rings, diamonds set in a gold band, engraved in the art deco style. Friends of my parents in England suggested that my mother sell the rings, given the debts, and her poor employment prospects. Her indignation knew no bounds. I doubt that she had ever worn the rings. Very gaudy, they were probably always meant as an investment against a rainy day rather than as jewelry to be displayed on one's finger. But surely this was a rainy day. Neither on this nor on the many other rainy days that followed did my mother sell the rings. Was it because the symbol of security provided more security than its actual exchange value? I prefer the more romantic reading. She loved my father her entire life, loved and deprecated him, loved and treated him cruelly. She would sometimes tell me of another suitor, in the mid-1930s, Georges, the engineer. As she sighed for the stability that the path not taken might have provided her, who could not tell that in reminiscing about Georges, she chose my father all over again? (Or am I fooling myself, and it is I who chose my father all over again?) That my father had chosen her over everyone else, I am not so sure, and neither was she. The rings were a his and her set, reminiscent of an engagement or marriage band, although my mother had a simple wedding band that she wore for years. Their monetary value was an assurance and reassurance, neither measurable nor exchangeable. Twenty-five years after my mother's death, I have repeated the pattern, not selling them even though retirement might dictate making profitable investments. The closest I have come is to ask friends for the names of reliable appraisers. But maybe it is not so puzzling. Do children sell their parents' wedding bands? What, in fact, happens to wedding bands?

Even more a sign of the topsy-turvy nature of measurable and unmeasurable was my mother's reaction to receiving a letter sent from Brussels, which contained a crisp one hundred dollar bill. It arrived not long after our move to the States. The sender, Madame Knoblauch, had not been a particularly close friend, but the couples had socialized. It touched my mother very much to receive this letter. I do not remember whether she was already dictating all her letters to me or whether she still wrote them herself. The few letters I received from her when I was in France, were filled with grammar and spelling mistakes. Answering Madame Knoblauch in Yiddish would not have solved the problem since she had no more formal instruction in it than she had in French. But I digress. The important point is that my mother never spent that one hundred dollars. I found it in her safety deposit box at her death.

I have caught myself doing something very similar recently. In emptying out my own safe deposit box, I found six one hundred-dollar bills, the remains of a sum of money my mother had set aside and into which I dipped during the year I took off from work when she was dying. I had completely forgotten about it. I have not spent those bills since, keeping them in the same envelope they had been in for the past quarter century. This makes even less sense than keeping jewelry whose only use is its monetary value, purchased expressly as security. At least one can see the symbolic meaning of a his and her ring set. But to take money itself, made out of paper, meant to be spent, as a talisman? Who does that? Many people, it turns out. What are all those framed bills doing on shop walls?

I take pleasure in these reversals, but sometimes they work in the other direction—the immeasurable turning into the measurable. My mother would often tell me, with a degree of exasperation unaffected by the passing of time, that my father had refused to apply for German reparations payment. He had spent three years in a German slave labor camp, and the year before that in a harsh transit camp in Compiègne, outside Paris. Obviously, that pension would have alleviated the precariousness of their circumstances. Decades later, when we were already in Los Angeles, my mother did apply to get some compensation, receiving a small lump sum, for loss of property. I had always sided with my father on this, and was uncomfortable when my mother proceeded with her request. We were not to benefit from the horror. Lately, I have come to see my mother's side as well. The compensation was for material damage, for the wages unpaid, for the objects stolen. It is a way of affirming that war does not obliterate the principle of justice and that perpetrators must pay. Seeing my mother's action in this light has not erased my respect for my father's choice. Accepting the compensation, if technically only for material damages, can unwittingly become blood money, slide into an equivalence between a human life and a quantity that makes good for its absence. My parents may have acted viscerally, my father in the early 1950s, with the war still so close, and my mother much later, in her old age, on all sorts of state assistance, not to mention mine. But it is not only a matter of visceral reactions to different historical moments. In the balance is the difference between a reasonable and an unreasonable unworldliness. But is unworldliness ever reasonable?

I am willing to concede that my contrast between worldliness and unworldliness is murky, not to say inadequate, in the face of the endless permutations of our relationship to wealth. But I am not willing to give up on the reality that touched me in my youth. Something great lay out there, for which one strove all one's life. Recently, in reading Camus's *The Plague*, I found a similar insistence. The narrator describes the Algerian city of Oran, before the plague, as a town in which everyone is busy making money and then spending it on leisure activities. Nothing is more natural, he says, than to see people working from morning till night and then playing cards and gossiping in cafes in the evening. "But there are cities and countries where, from time to time, people suspect that there is something else. Generally, it does not change their life. Still, there had been a suspicion of something else, and that is already an achievement."[1] In the age of the billionaires, it might be worth trying to recapture, from many different angles, what that something was.

---

1    Albert Camus, *La Peste* (Paris: Éditions Gallimard, 1947), 12 (my translation); Albert Camus, *The Plague*, trans. Stuart Gilbert (New York: The Modern Library, 1948), 4.

# 6

# Russian Friendships

My mother, who ended up spending much of her life alone, would often reminisce about my father's circle of friends. I learned their names early, each with an accompanying epithet: Boris of the impressive physique, the volleyball champion; Edgar, of the quiet demeanor, the artist who never married; Nahum of the overflowing goodness, who left potatoes for my mother during the war. All had been Russian-speaking Jewish immigrants to Paris, and among them only Boris escaped being deported to the camps. He is also the only one I got to know as an adult. The others, including my father, died young, leaving me only childhood memories. One of these memories involves Edgar. He had come to visit us in Brussels, after my father died. Knowing that he was an artist, I cajoled him into contributing to my autograph album. In my Brussels elementary school, none of us cared a whit for the heartfelt sentiments contributors inscribed on the left side of the page, as long as on the right side they produced a drawing or painting that we could show off to our classmates. Edgar spent hours on his, a marvel of detail and shading, a family of ants, dressed up in formal clothing, and an ant dog in a little dog house, among many other details. It was a masterpiece. Maybe because he was in a hurry to catch his train back to Paris, he never wrote the few words on the opposite side, leaving the drawing without even his name. He died not long afterward. Today, almost sixty years later, that blank page on the other side occupies me much more than the drawing. I am indebted, with no way to get out of debt. I can only recall those debts to my parents' friends, describing how I incurred them.

Edgar's drawing in my autograph book.

## Boris

I first met Boris when he came to visit us in Brussels from Paris. It may have been from him that I received the children's version of *The Three Musketeers*, a book whose depiction of the four dashing French swordsmen must have blended seamlessly with my mother's tales of the four Russian Jews of her youth. D'Artagnan, Athos, Portos, Aramis—Yasha, Boris, Nahum, Edgar. My first real memory of Boris dates to a later visit, at my father's first *yahrzeit*, the one-year anniversary of his death. My mother, he and I went to the cemetery, my only visit until my return to it forty eight years later. It was a sunny day. I skipped and sang. My mother, not a perspicacious reader of the child mind, reproached me my abyss of unfeeling. In the year that I got to know Boris, during my stay in France as a student in 1972-1973, he expressed surprise that I survived my mother's upbringing. He hadn't bet on it, he told me. It is difficult to remember how I reacted to this. No doubt it legitimated my self-pity. Why was my mother not more like Boris and Renée, his wife? When their youngest son, still a teenager, did not sleep at home on some nights, they just assumed he was at his girlfriend's. "Il a découché," Boris would tell me with an indulgent smile. My mother, on the other hand, when I had come home late one evening, was so convinced that my friend at the time had done unspeakable things that she chased him down the path of our apartment building with a broom.

Boris, far left, Edgar, my mother and father, my cousin Haney.
Woman sitting unknown.

I acknowledge that the broom scene is unusual. But most children survive much worse. They have to. Taken from the opposite angle, what does "having survived" really mean? It is always a very partial affair, this business of growing up, of maintaining mental balance, something Boris must have seen in my anxious and very tentative ways of that year. I remember being extremely self-conscious about making a salad dressing at his house. Renée, his wife, was impatient with me. What is this? Her children divided their support between Trotsky and Mao, and I limited my concerns to salad dressings? Perhaps Boris, in telling me that I had survived, was trying to reassure me about my future. I was going to make it, despite occasional mishaps. I have to report that I now make a very good salad dressing, almost universally praised, freeing me up for the higher realms.

Boris's evaluation of my mother was, in general, very harsh. She was a fair-weather wife, he told me once, good to my father when things were going well and cruel to him when their finances sank. He had often advised my father to divorce her but my father would not do it, Boris would sigh. Again, I have absolutely no idea of how I took this statement at the time. I know that it had never entered my mind that my parents could have divorced. It happened to no one I knew personally, only to film actors. The world must have shifted a little, introducing hitherto unimagined possibilities.

Today, I weigh the justice of Boris's assessment of my mother. She had indeed often complained about money. An event in the remote past, while my parents still lived in France, long before the two years of my father's unemployment in Warsaw, and the two years of employment in Brussels, would occasionally rise in her memory. He had won a large sum of money in Monte-Carlo, and then continued to bet until he lost it, against everyone's advice. In Warsaw and Brussels, she reproached him for always footing all the bills at restaurants, as if he still had the money to host all his friends and acquaintances when he did not have a salary. The list went on. I always secretly sided with my father in these matters, reacting to my mother's nagging as violence against his person. It must be admitted, however, that when my father died, he left my mother not only penniless but also in debt, with a child to take care of in the bargain. Beyond this, Boris seemed to have been completely blind to another source of her heartache. He had told me that my father had had a lifelong love, and that it was not my mother, but Boris's sister. Both had married, but it did not spell the end of their relationship.

In the stories that my mother had told me about Boris, she had mentioned that he had been a great womanizer. His long-suffering wife Renée would say. "Don't you worry. In old age, he will make a good husband." As far as I could see, in old-age Boris did make a good husband, affectionately calling his wife "little bandit," taking pleasure in her no-nonsense ways and her no-nonsense shoes. My mother had presented Renée's attitude without comment, as if the moral of the tale lay in its very telling. The one significant clue was that Renée, unlike the other Jewish wives and girlfriends, was French. I understood from this that Renée's longue durée view of infidelity was a local curiosity. The universal pattern, my mother knew, was hurt, jealousy and vindictiveness. She was right. But I wish also that she had not been cruel to my father, the nagging about money being the least of it. I often suspect that her cruelty ate away at her after he died. Why else would she have accused me of having killed him? If she had rheumatism, she would take one look at my fingers and detect its first signs in me. If she felt she had done something wrong, I must have done something equivalent or worse. I did not subscribe to this physics of entanglement, even in childhood, but the whole saga does leave one a bit confused. I suspected, for instance, that neither waiting it out or lashing out was the proper response to love betrayed, but could only grope in the dark for the freeing alternative. Even in adulthood, I continue groping.

I did meet Boris's sister in that fateful year of 1972-1973, on her visit from Israel. She was a beautiful and elegant woman. My mother had also been beautiful and elegant, but after a decade of resistance, had finally given in to the ill-fitting polyester clothing of the LA neighborhood we lived in. In her mid-fifties at the time, her shoulders were already beginning to stoop, and her hair, dyed a nondescript brown, sat neatly teased in a halo on her head. Boris's sister, whose white hair waved gracefully around her face, and who was very kind to me, has stayed in my mind. But she did not really displace my mother in my imagination of my father's affections, never taking on the role that Boris said she had had. That one visit was too little to go on to change the many details of my parents' relationships that I did know.

Boris's revelation of my father's great love did serve one useful purpose. Given my mother's frequent misinterpretations of the motives of those around her, I might have concluded that in her accusations of infidelity, she had been wrong once again. And, indeed, some of her suspicions in Brussels were completely off the mark. Even a seven-year old could see that the heavyset Mme. Kalichmann was not the object of my father's interests. Had my mother known about Boris's sister? If she did, she never mentioned it. I think she did know. Boris's sister and her husband had lived in Vienna for a while after the war, one of the sites of my father's business trips during our time in Poland. Was the beautiful silver necklace with light-blue stones that he brought back from one of those visits a guilt offering? I wear it very infrequently, vague intimations of Viennese trysts wafting around my neck.

I must insist that it is only now that I look askance at Boris's judgments. When I was twenty, the content of his revelations lay, first and foremost, in the intimacy they created. We would walk arm-in-arm in the streets of Paris, his French lurching in spurts of high and low notes against the background of a Russian melody, and I would be my father's daughter. I looked like my mother, so much so, in fact, that once, much later, when I went to meet some old Yiddish actors in a Paris community center, one of them, upon seeing me, spontaneously uttered my mother's name. Różka! It had been fifty years since he had last seen her. With Boris, I was not exclusively my mother's daughter. He welcomed into his home the same man whom my mother had chased with a broom. Later, when Geoffrey exited the picture of his own accord, Jérôme and I stayed overnight with Boris before our trip to the Pyrenees. As I shivered under the freezing water of the shower the morning of our departure, I imagined, with a certain joy, the rigors of the camping life ahead. My father had given me my initial swimming lessons, had begun to teach me how to ride a bike, had given me figure skating lessons just before his heart attack. My mother, on the other hand, would often have me walk on the inside of the street, afraid some car might suddenly hop onto the sidewalk. With Boris, I walked carefree, or at least knew it might be possible.

Boris died of a stroke at the very end of that year. The telegram reached us in the Pyrenees where I was helping Jérôme tend sheep. I sobbed without restraint, relieved, in a dim way, by the flow of tears. When I returned to Paris, I brought back the sleeping bag Boris and Renée had lent me. Not finding anyone at home, I left it with a note on their doorstep. With Renée, I never got in touch again. She had never liked me. I suppose I also did not like her much. She was too practical, too competent, too matter of fact. I mean to say that she did not share Boris's sense of death-defying friendship.

## Pola

From my mother's stories, I also knew that, of my father's friends, Nahum had been her favorite. There was something about his gift of a sack of potatoes that had moved her deeply. It was a gesture of concern for her in very hard times, but also expressed something characteristic of him, a very rare gentle putting himself out for others, as if there were no other way to be. Nahum, his wife Pola and his son did come to visit us in Brussels. It must have been around 1958 because he died two years before my father. The only part of his visit that I remember resembles a scene from an old black and white movie. My mother and he are sitting in the back seat of what must have been an ample taxi. I was an extra on the set, with a nonspeaking part, sitting in the taxi as well, but visible only to the camera, and not to the two protagonists, absorbed in each other. He and she exchanged words of parting. The air was filled with a longing that could not be fulfilled. My mother never talked about this, and it is possible that this scene is the product of my overheated child's imagination.

Once we got to the States, my mother would dictate letters to Pola, Nahum's wife. They were quite formulaic, usually written on the major holidays. The fact that she insisted on sending them was a sign of how much she valued the friendship. Given the infrequency and expense of air travel in those days, it was very unlikely that the women would ever see each other again. The bond my mother was expressing through her correspondence may not have been with Pola alone, although my mother liked and deeply trusted Pola. It was a bond with that circle of friends of the war years and beyond. It was also an expression of gratitude. Pola was among the friends who had helped us financially after my father's death.

When I met Pola in that fateful year of 1972-1973, I loved her right away. She managed to make a space for me in that tiny, tiny apartment, in which every corner served three purposes and the telephone never worked. Invisible rules were involved, but she also gave herself, along with the rules. I knew it. The chief rule is that without extravagance, there was no gift. Her standards of hospitality were impossibly high, requiring that she cook elaborate meals for me, a twenty-year-old, and cede her own bed even when Marc, her son, was not home, and I could have slept on the sofa in the dining room, his bed, for the couple of days I stayed with them. She was already around sixty that year, and I would protest. She would not hear of it. She did not expect extravagance in return. The rule was to keep the giving unequal, with the balance on her side. But I was keenly aware that some reciprocity, albeit symbolic, was required. To figure how this could be done involved quite a bit of mental gymnastics, and occasionally led to grief. I was not altogether new at this kind of exercise, although with Pola it involved special training. I did not mind the special training. Pola, like Nahum in my mother's stories, was, despite the complications, someone who put herself out because that was the human way to be.

Pola Strechinsky and her grandson.

In Boris's household, a small house at the outskirts of Paris, a certain bohemian style of living prevailed. Pola, on the other hand, had something of the lady to the manor born. Despite her very modest dwelling, she had come from a well-off family in Bessarabia, and both she and Nahum had pursued a university education, although I am not sure she was able to complete hers, given the war. She was aware of levels of language, praising this or that interlocutor for their *français châtié*, their impeccable French. She herself spoke un français chatié, despite the soft Russian "t" that accompanied her pronunciation of the word *châtié*. That first year of our acquaintance her son was seriously involved with a tall, blond, aristocratic French woman who rode horses. Pola was adamantly against her. Marc could bring home anyone, and she listed all the impermissible categories that she would accept anyway, but not this woman. She had not taken off her long white gloves to shake Pola's hands. How could anyone be so dismissive of someone else? Marc eventually did break off that relationship. Although I asked, he never explained. I am not convinced that Pola had anything to do with it. Marc was a god and he knew he could do whatever he wanted without risking demotion. On the other hand, even divinities relent and show mercy occasionally. For very different reasons, for a long time Pola also disliked the woman who eventually became Marc's wife. Some months before her death, she apologized to Évelyne. It was a very emotional moment, the retelling of that scene, with Pola bleeding uncontrollably from an illness she refused to have diagnosed, and Évelyne tending to her against her will.

Pola, despite her good breeding, was incorrigibly superstitious. My mother would recall that if you complimented her on how handsome her little Marc was, she would immediately deny it, loudly call him ugly, or invent another negative trait on the spot to thwart the evil eye. When I took over the friendship some twenty years later, Pola cautioned me against placing Jérôme's hat on her bed because it could spell harm for him, smiling knowingly when I hastily removed it. She also upheld the more well-known interdiction regarding umbrellas—not to be opened inside the house for the bad luck this would bring. In this one area, my mother, who stemmed from a lower social class than Pola's but who did not share these customs, could show indulgence from on high. It is not certain, however, that Pola would have characterized her behavior as superstitious. These were tried and true precautions against the evil eye, the evidence for whose existence was overwhelming.

From her perspective the one true superstition was religion, the existence of the divinity at its center lacking the same level of certainty. She did not have Marc circumcised, she told me, because what do modern people have to do with such backward practices? In Pola's mind, leaving Judaism had nothing to do with blending into a nondescript universalism, however. The line between Jews and Frenchmen remained very strong. The French, she would say, excel at decorating store windows, among the many other things they excelled at. Once at a dinner that her daughter-in-law had prepared, to which Pola insisted on bringing half the food, and to which my friend Paul and I had been invited, she graciously asked that Paul carve the roast, a specialty of the French people, she proclaimed. Despite the pressure to preserve the national honor, he executed himself admirably, proving her point. I was quite used to these demarcations, having heard a similar way of drawing lines all my life. I trotted out a comparison between Jews and Frenchmen of my own at a lunch given by some of Paul's friends, who were Jewish. I would probably be very embarrassed today to recall what exactly I had said, in my mind an innocuous witticism. Afterward, Paul reprimanded me. Olivier and his family might be Jewish, but his father was no less than a general in the French army. Did I not understand how offensive I had been, implying that he was not French? I had not understood. For me, you could be perfectly French in a thousand ways, and there could also be a line between Jew and Frenchman. But logic fails in such circumstances. I knew better for the future, avoiding such remarks in the presence of French generals.

Since Pola and I came to know each other over a fifteen-year period, the conversation often veered away from my parents. But occasionally, they would appear. My father, she told me, was an artist by vocation, unsuited to the political life. Unlike Boris, she never said anything overtly critical about my mother, although she would sometimes rectify what she felt was my wrong impression of her. Once I mentioned a story my mother had told me about her behavior after all the husbands in her circle had been arrested and in transit camps. She had been the one to organize food packages and to bring them to Compiègne, when the other wives had been slow to act, a sign of her courage. Your mother was as scared as the rest of us, Pola said gently. At another point, when I was remarking on how beautiful my mother had been in her youth, Pola interrupted me. You are as beautiful as she was, she told me. I was taken aback. I had not realized that I was comparing myself to her. In my mind, my mother was beautiful and that was that. Given the rush of pleasure I experienced when Pola made her remark, it might not have been so simple.

My mother in the 1930s.

Here, I must open a long parenthesis in defense of my mother, even if Pola's remark was not intended critically. If I was surprised by her remark, it was not because my mother made me feel physically unattractive. Her specialty lay more in the moral realm. Thinking back on it, though, when my parents still had the means in Poland, my mother went on a veritable rampage of corrective interventions, and all before I turned seven. She had me wear special shoes for flat feet, sent me to a music school to correct my tone deafness, and to an eye doctor for uncrossing my eyes, which resulted in decades of prescription eye glasses. I had none of these conditions, but my mother's exertions may have worked as a kind of amulet, preventing them from developing. I do regret that my time in the tone-deaf school was so brief. I was not tone-deaf but perhaps I could have reached unheard of heights of musical ability. My mother did not aim to make me a child prodigy, however. She aimed to raise me to the level of normalcy.

As I grew into adulthood, my mother took exception not to my external appearance but to my inattention to it. She was right about my general neglect, partially the result of the style of the late '60s and early '70s, or at least my interpretation of the natural look that style required. She wished I took better care of my clothing, that I wore some make-up, that I develop some coquettishness. She was still of the generation that did not go out without putting a little dash of this, and a touch of that on her face, a sign that one was in public, although this cannot be reduced to a generational matter. I was, more likely, part of an enclave of make-up-free innocents within my cohort. My refusal of make-up was not purely a matter of principle, however. I lacked skill. The few times I tried, the eyeliner ran, causing dark circles, the lipstick smudged etc. Paul once urged me to put some on. He was an artist, and since we were meeting with an important gallery owner, he wanted my face to reflect the official nature of the occasion. I complied, complaining all the while that I now looked feverish. It doesn't matter, he replied. At least you intend to look that way. It was not only my mother whom I frustrated with the authenticity of my appearance.

To her credit, she did by and large practice a quiet resignation in the later years. Once, when I visited her in the retirement home, noticing that I looked pale, she asked me if my conviction that I was a natural beauty prevented me from wearing lipstick. But her heart was not in it anymore, I could tell. She was aiming just to see whether she could still hit the mark. We laughed. On Melrose Avenue, not far from her retirement home, on one of our walks we had stepped into a store. I tried on a pair of earrings, and after much hesitation, decided against buying them. "She is historian," my mother explained to the young saleswoman, sure that she would grasp the full relevance of my profession to my otherwise inexplicable choice.

Pola, beyond the one remark that led to this long digression, never commented on my appearance again. Of my relations with my admirers, though, she occasionally took a very stern view. I once permitted myself a little fit of hysteria, responding to an early version of being stuck, at least in my mind, between two interested parties. One had asked me to go to Holland and the other somewhere else. What to do? I broke down, crying loudly that I had made an irrevocably bad choice. It was unseemly to behave this way, Pola responded, devoid of all sympathy for my plight. Although she did not like what she took for exhibitionism, an emotionalism so little contained in the proper form, I think she liked my divided heart even less. She was the very image of wholeness in love, going month after month, year after year to her husband's grave to speak to him, devoting every fiber of her being for Marc, even including me within the circle of those to whom one gave unstintingly.

The last time I saw Pola, she insisted that we go shopping together at Marks and Spencer. She wanted to buy me a gift. As the ritual required, I protested three times, quite sincerely, that I did not need anything, and desisted the fourth time, as was also required. I wore the product of that expedition, a beige and pink camisole, very simple and very feminine, for many years. At the street corner, we parted. She looked at me, her brown eyes and rueful smile telling me that we would not see each other again. I pretended I did not catch the message. A few months later, when the announcement of her death arrived, I sobbed uncontrollably, just as I had done for Boris. A year or so later, her daughter-in-law showed me letters that Pola had kept for half a century, her correspondence with Nahum when they were separated for a period of time before the war. I did not read much of it. My visit with Marc and Évelyne was too short for a longer perusal, made even shorter by the fact that the letters were in Russian. In the little that I did read, Pola and Nahum's tenderness, and the superfluous giving so natural to them, wafted across time and space.

As I have often said, my mother's judgment of the people around her could be tragically off the mark. But when it came to those friendships of long ago, she was right to the tenth decimal point. I have repeated the experiment.

# Theological Fragments

Late at night, a snippet of what I had read in a *New Yorker* article came back to me. Adam Gopnik had been reflecting on a literary topic—the genre of the aphorism. In his elegant overview, the term stretched to include parables, sutras, midrashim, hadith, the central modes of expression of religious traditions. Like the pithy saying we associate with the aphorism, all favor a short form, a fragment that does not attempt to become more than a glimpse. Of course, what I saw in my mind's eye was not the exact quotation below but it is this quotation that gave rise to whatever I did see.

> The more mystical appraisal of the aphorism is that the fragment captures all we can hope to see of the divine. Our universe and the God within it are too big to be systematized; we can see Him or Her most clearly in glimpses, the way ants see humans.[1]

For Gopnik, "the mystical appraisal of the aphorism" is one explanation among others. More practical accounts for the aphorism's existence argue for the shortness of our attention span. The fragment, on this reading, would be a clever way to reach the majority of people, incapable of more extended concentration. I marvel at Gopnik's bonhomie. For me, to say that we can grasp the universe and God, the whole and the source of the whole, only in glimpses, is not a neutral proposition. It is a battle cry. We are promised daily that in just a few years artificial intelligence will not only duplicate the functions of the human mind but also improve upon them; we are promised that biology and related sciences will discover the genetic code of, say, all diseases and of all criminal behavior and that a cure for both ills is within sight. These are not

---

1  Adam Gopnik, "Brevity, Soul, Wit. The Art of the Aphorism," *The New Yorker*, July 22, 2019.

mere rhetorical flourishes but turn into gigantic, often state-supported research programs whose results lead to our increasing vulnerability to external manipulation and design. It annoyed me that such questions were too ponderous for Gopnik's urbane and graceful wit. But why should he see what I see? Why should he be me?

As I was engaging in this internal monologue, trying to figure out what had so miffed me in an otherwise charming and instructive article, I suddenly had one of those insights that seemed so crystal clear that I fell asleep elated, not even bothering to jot down notes, confident that something would stay with me until morning. Something did stay with me, but unfortunately, it shared the fate of most insights that come in the middle of the night, pale in comparison to the original epiphany. But a wan insight is still an insight, and so I proceed: the experience of a reality that we catch briefly but cannot hold is part of everyone's daily life. I feel compelled to capture that ungraspable dimension at the heart of our ordinary encounters through fragments of my own. What else, if not the ungraspable, is worth the effort?

## Fragment 1—Unlocking and Locking

Once, when my mother was already very quiet and none too steady on her feet, I took her for a short ride to a neighboring park. We got out of the car and walked a little amid the foliage. She leaned on me. We made our way slowly. Out of the blue, she asked, "Do you believe there is a world we go to after we die? Will we see each other again?" For decades, we had talked about the most daily things. This person had said that to that person. You ate this and I ate that. Tomorrow we need to do such and such. In the last two years of her life, I had done most of the talking, and usually only at the beginning of my visits. The rest of the time, I would sit by her side, reading a book, or lie down next to her for a while. That is all that seemed possible. I knew her general mood, which rarely varied. I knew she could sense mine. But I did not know what she was thinking beneath the silence. She never asked the questions in the park again. A world submerged under our daily exchanges appeared and disappeared.

As if one story were not sufficient to make the point, I offer a second one, almost redundant but what can be redundant if the submerged world the story aims to reach is inexhaustible? During one of my visits to her in the psychiatric ward, my mother told me she had just seen my father in a dream. She asked him to stop seeing other women. It made her feel so worthless, she explained to him. If he could not stop, he would have to leave. Her voice was soft as she related this to me. Twenty-eight years after my father's death, her rage was spent, but not her sorrow. When I had described her mental illness in a previous chapter, I had mentioned that she was not capable of analyzing herself in the terms required by the therapy of the time. She had remained silent in the face of the hospital psychiatrist's questions. But, yes, she knew that she felt as if she were nothing. She knew it had something to do with her relationship to my father, what she did or did not say to him. Perhaps the right person at the right moment could have had access to that impregnable fortress. The inability to find the key to another person at the very moment we are communicating might be the most common, daily elusiveness. Yet, as my mother's few sentences about her dream testify, a fragment opens out into a world, in its own time.

## Fragment 2: Emptying and Overflowing

In the spring of 1975, my second semester of graduate school, Kees assigned a very difficult text that I was to present to our seminar. I read it and reread it, but I could not catch the thread—my effort was so great that my mind froze. Thoughts dissolved into unconnected sentences, and the sentences into mere sound. After hours of trying to break the spell, I began to hit my head against the wall of my room. Since I was all of twenty-three at the time, and not a child, the violence of my behavior startled me back to my senses. Okay, nothing to be done, I will not present this text to the seminar. I cannot spend the rest of my life going around banging my head against walls. The next day, to my relief, I started writing gingerly, careful to avoid the heights. It was the first paper I wrote on Emmanuel Levinas, about whom I continued to write for many years, and whose thought is not incidental to the theme of this chapter.

Almost ten years later, in my first year of full-time teaching, I was preparing a class the way I had done many times before. It was late in the academic year. I had taught this particular book some years back but had never liked it. Committed to finding a sympathetic way in, I tried for hours until my mind froze up again, dislocating sentence from sense. Already quite late at night, I called Kees, who recommended I take two aspirins with hot milk, which I dutifully proceeded to do. The next morning, to my discomfiture, nothing had changed. In class, I said something to the students. The students said something back. Nothing connected to anything else. I cancelled my afternoon sessions. There was nothing to do but to quit teaching. I went home. A friendly colleague, aware of my distress, came over to distract me, chatting about her love life. I distinctly remember that, although married, she was in love with a gay man. I had never heard of this situation before. When she left, I sat down to write my letter of resignation to the director of my program but found myself preparing the loathed text instead. It was Freud's *Civilization and Its Discontents*, I am embarrassed to say. It was as if I had had a twenty-four-hour flu of the mind, an explanation the great master would have found beneath contempt. I continued to teach for another thirty-four years. As happens with many teachers, a nervous flutter preceded every class but the experience of utter dislocation did not occur again.

The term "panic attack" was not in wide circulation in those years. But undoubtedly I had panicked and undoubtedly it had been an attack. Today, I would rather view these incidents through the lens of "pride" and "humility," words as unlikely to have come to my mind in the 1970s and 1980s as "panic attack." I was content and discontent to be a neurotic. In both instances of the mind freeze, I had reached too high, wanted too much—pride, all the way down. In the fall from grace that followed—my utter incapacity to function—I regained (who knows how?) the proper relationship between desiring and letting go, if only temporarily. How does that balance happen? There are techniques—breathing, praying, meditation. But if so, what do the words "pride" and "humility" add? We can just sit and meditate, stilling the breath and the mind. Is not simply understanding the mechanism of how to calm anxiety enough? Maybe. But with the notions of pride and humility, we become seekers of a good. Attaining it requires desisting from pursuing it in the wrong way. Pride and humility express the metaphysic of desire, and an ethical sensibility, that the term panic attack, so ethically flat and physiological, does not. But our inner lives are full of that movement of desire, reaching and letting go, and reaching again. These are the elusive movements of every day, which we hardly even register, except in crisis cases. We live so much within them that we do not notice. Maybe the people we call mystics do notice them, recording moments of grasping, emptying, and overflowing.

## Fragment 3: Irony and Miracle

I propose here to read a short story, an aphorism as Gopnik presents it, whose point, as I see it, is precisely to direct our attention to moments of overflow in our encounter with others. The story, I. B. Singer's "Piece of Advice" is very sly in the way it makes this point, leaving us in doubt as to whether it even makes it. But why should the literature that reaches for something too big to catch be less elusive than its subject?

"A Piece of Advice" seems at first to have nothing elusive about it. Its moral is spelled out in blazing colors in the words of the holy man, the rebbe of Kuzmir, whose miraculous powers the story showcases. We cannot change our emotions at will, he teaches, but we can change our behavior. Eventually, a change of habit will lead to a change of heart. "What should a Jew do if he is not a pious man. . . . Let him play the pious man. . . . Are you angry perhaps? Go ahead and be angry, but speak gentle words and be friendly at the same time."[2] The plot illustrates the rebbe's wisdom. The chief protagonist of the story, a well-to-do, observant Jew, is extremely irritated whenever things do not go his way, abusing others both verbally and physically. He even goes so far as to slap his own son-in-law, the narrator of "A Piece of Advice," in front of the entire family. Learned in Jewish sources, the father-in-law knows this behavior is shameful since the rabbis underscore its full severity in many places. "Better to throw oneself in a fiery furnace than to shame another person publicly."[3] "Anyone who publicly mortifies his companion is akin to a shedder of blood."[4] No matter how well aware of this he may be, he still does not succeed in controlling his fits of anger. On his son-in-law's advice, he agrees to visit the above mentioned rebbe of Kuzmir, a holy man who might heal him. The fact that he consents suggests the depth of his despair. He is a Misnaged, an opponent of the holy men of the Hasidic movement, considering them all to be charlatans, and, to this point, never shy about expressing his contempt.[5]

Initially, the father-in-law's meeting with the rebbe only confirms his judgment. He is told that whenever he is on the verge of heaping abuse on someone, he should pay the person at the source of his irritation compliments for a week in a row. This is hypocrisy, the father-in-law fumes. Holy men are all ignoramuses, unfamiliar with Jewish teachings. Why else would they advise replacing one sin with another which is just as bad if not worse? Because of Shabbat, he is forced to spend another day in the rebbe's company, during which he has occasion to observe the latter's interactions with his disciples, how he prays and preaches. Before leaving, he agrees to one more private audience with the holy

---

2   Isaac Bashevis Singer, "A Piece of Advice," in *Collected Stories: Gimpel the Fool to the Letter Writer*, ed. Ilan Stavans (New York: Library of America, 2004), 269.
3   *Babylonian Talmud*, Sotah 10b.
4   Ibid., Bava Metziah 58b.
5   Singer is reproducing here the conflict between these two branches of the Jewish tradition, Hasidism and its opponents, the Misnagdim, present in his own family. These branches arose in the mid-to late eighteenth century in Eastern Europe and continue to the present day.

man. This time, the miracle happens. He changes. With great difficulty, he sets about speaking kindly to all who infuriate him. "And if the water carrier splashed water entering our house, though I knew this just about drove my father-in-law crazy, he never showed it. 'How are you, Reb Yontle?' 'Are you cold, eh?' One could feel that he did this only with great effort. That's what made it noble." [6] Eventually, the father-in-law stops feeling anger altogether, becoming so kind that he turns into a holy man himself. The narrator concludes with a resounding endorsement of the rebbe's advice, extending it even further. "If you are not happy, act the happy man. Happiness will come later. So also with faith. If you are in despair, act as though you believed. Faith will come afterward."[7] The point is glaringly clear.

Elusiveness nonetheless enters the story, not through the plot, but in the details of *how* it is told. The Hasidic son-in-law, the narrator, is a comical character. So absorbed is he in Torah study that he cannot be bothered with the details of physical existence. He tells us, as if this were perfectly natural, that he regularly mistakes someone else's house for the one in which he lives with his wife's family. "Doesn't my father-in-law live here?" he would ask.[8] When he does notice his physical surroundings, he sees transcendent meaning everywhere. A snow-covered landscape signifies the merging of heaven and earth, a poetic image that many might use but for the narrator it is not mere metaphor. The fact that snow is white, and that an older man's beard also turns white hints at a profound unity beneath appearances. White is the sign of mercy, he adds.[9] In his rebbe's prayer house, he departs into oneness and mercy altogether, leaving the physical world behind. During one Friday night service, he prayed with such enthusiasm that, "I was no longer Baruch from Rachev—but bodiless, sheer nothing." [10] His body, in the meantime, is kept alive by his worldly father-in-law, a fact to which Baruch attributes no significance whatsoever.

The narrator's proclivity to leave ordinary reality for the sake of a deeper one is not altogether unconnected to his penchant for exaggeration. The bread he ate in his childhood home was always at least two weeks old, so hard that it had to be dipped in water first, he tells us. When he was young, snow was not today's snow. Back then, it fell for a month without stopping. We should also

---

6   Singer, *Collected Stories*, 270-271.
7   Ibid., 271.
8   Ibid., 266.
9   Ibid., 267.
10  Ibid., 269.

consider how the story begins. "Talk about a holy man! Our powers are not theirs; their ideas are not for us to understand. But let me tell you what happened to my father-in-law."[11] This identifies his narrative as a Hasidic wonder tale, a genre with more than a hint of hyperbole, since it is often told not only to brag about the superiority of one's own holy man vis-a-vis others, but also to persuade the opponents, the Misnagdim, of the wrong approach of cold rationalism alone. The father-in-law, a rich and powerful Misnaged, cannot lay claim to the infinitely greater power of a Hasidic rebbe.

The presence of this idiosyncratic narrator might account for the whiff of irony lacing "A Piece of Advice." Irony plays between appearance and reality, as is well known. It becomes quite possible that Singer's message is the very opposite of the one the narrator so praises. If you think that it is sufficient to act happy to be happy, that it is possible to change one's habits against the grain of one's passions, you are as naive and as unworldly as Baruch from Rachev. According to this reading, the advice the rebbe gives is glib, and the evidence for its success very slim. We would all be happy and gentle by now. It is equally possible, however, that Singer's irony is directed not at the narrator but at his enlightened readers, those who, like himself, had left the Jewish religious tradition behind. For this group, claims to having witnessed a miracle merely signify credulity and charlatanism. There is no transcendent force interrupting the material world. If looked at more closely, every so-called miracle can be explained through the laws of nature, which account for everything. But what if Baruch is right in affirming that miracles do occur? How does it happen that one person influences another, to the point of setting him or her on a path to profound transformation? We do not know. It was not the technique the rebbe prescribed that, in itself, did the trick. It was the rebbe.

Within the framework of the Hasidic tradition, a human being's ability to deflect pride into humility, to touch the basic spring of our internal makeup, cannot be explained through a list of causes. It happens in an inexplicable way, thus accounting for the rebbe's holy status, since he becomes a vehicle for a power transcending our causal explanations. To understand as a miracle the influence for the good that one person exerts on another is not devoid of humor. It assumes that any fundamental improvement in our character can only be an act of divine intervention, akin to the splitting of the Red Sea. It sounds like a joke. But without ceasing to be a joke, it may also be serious. The change the rebbe initiated in the father-in-law depends on an

---

11 Ibid., 264.

interaction that cannot be duplicated. Not every rebbe will do and not every father-in-law will do. Two specific people interacted at a specific moment, and a great change occurred. Why would this not be a miracle? The only reason we refuse this term as a proper description of these events is that they occur without fanfare, in the movements of the heart in our daily life. The surface ordinariness masks the extraordinary nature of the change. Stories such as "A Piece of Advice," capture this effect of one person on another. But the irony remains. Is there an overflow in some of our interactions or are we merely exaggerating if we claim this? The irony preserves the elusiveness of the influence of another person. It is not one thing, and maybe it is nothing at all.

I love "A Piece of Advice" for this elusiveness. I have spent a long time turning it this way and that, seeing a different nuance, a different possibility each time, only some of which I have recorded here. It allows me to return to daily interactions of my own, and try my hand at my insight of the middle of the night one last time, for now.

## In the Image of God

My friend Paul observed that his mother, so sincere in her hope that she and her deceased husband, would reunite after her own death, stopped making any reference to God, afterlife etc. in her declining years, as she sank into senility. He concluded that the part of the psyche oriented toward an invisible realm, seemingly so firmly entrenched, is likely to be the first to go. I have witnessed similar erasures among those around me. An elderly Protestant minister with whom I was close for three decades, steeped in the Calvinist tradition, stopped referring to anything Christian at all in the last year of his life. I explicitly asked him about it, but he refused to use any of the typical vocabulary—faith, hope, love—talking instead about a Japanese maple he wanted to have planted on the premises of the retirement complex, as a mute sign that he and his wife had once passed through this earth. There was nothing else, he said. Most surprising of all to me was the case of my friend Pien, who went to morning Mass for at least thirty years. She had once explained to me that for her it was a daily renewal, and it was clear to all who knew her that she was indeed privy to a vitality unwavering in its constancy. For her, its source lay in the Eucharist. In her last years, not only did her church attendance stop, which might have been partially a practical matter, but she also stopped referring to it, stopped desiring it. One could conclude that in the face of old age, disease, and death, a salvific realm beyond our senses reveals itself to be an illusion.

I see it otherwise. The same Protestant friend who refused any conversation on Christian themes clung fiercely to my hand when I would come visit, talking to me about all sorts of intimate matters. It is as if intimacy were all he desired and all he wanted to know. In his gesture, I hear the echo of my mother's questions in the park—Is there another world? Will we see each other again—arising out of a desire to perpetuate a bond, expressing the bond while longing for it. I conclude that our thirst for and response to a human presence remains, even if we make no reference to God, transcendence, the infinite. We continue to long for the overflowing reality of another person, the ground from which all these abstract words emanate. I would not be the first to understand their origin in this way, nor will I be the last. It goes back far, after all. What else would it mean to say that human beings are created in the image of God? Was the name "God," there first, or was the human being there first, prompting the author of the Book of Genesis to find the name, not for the human being, but for that overflow passing through? People of all times and places have fallen short when they babble about this too much. Best to stick to fragments—short stories and sutras and midrashim and even anecdotes about parents. This does not mean that every fragment is artful, thus repeating on the esthetic level the ethical mystery of why this person and not that one can profoundly influence another.

I am fully aware that stressing this level of our interactions with one another—its transcendent dimension, the overflow—makes me like the narrator of "A Piece of Advice," seeing in the whiteness of the snow the peace of heaven rather than a property explainable through snow's chemical composition. Was not my friend's clinging to my hand or my mother's questions in the park just an expression of the fear of dying, an instinctive reaction? Can we not account for the influence of one person on another through sociological and psychological factors? One might argue, for instance, that my insistence on transcendence is simply the result of being the daughter of a luftmentsch, who saw in the distance the brotherhood of all human beings, when close up there was nothing but horror. No wonder that I too see transcendence in unlikely places. I do not discount this possibility. Neither do I take it to negate the reality of what my father saw. I dedicate these theological reflections to him, but also to my mother, whose father visited a rebbe from time to time.

As to the self-evidence of that insight in the middle of the night, I can only say with Pascal, "A thought has escaped me: I was trying to write it down: instead I write that it escaped me."[12]

---

12 Blaise Pascal, "*Pensées*," trans. A. J. Krailsheimer (London: Penguin Books, 1995), 190.

# Postscript
# Talking to Myself about
# Literature

Doubts assail me. Memoirs, if they are worth their salt, aim to be literature. I am embarrassed to admit that I have not extirpated from my consciousness the Eastern European notion that only someone with the gifts of a Tolstoy is entitled to produce literature. Of course, in the famous Hasidic story, Rav Zusya, on Judgment Day will be asked, not if he had been Moses, but if he had been Rav Zusya. Chekhov once encouraged a writer, who too was afraid that he was not Tolstoy: "There are big dogs and little dogs, but little dogs must not fret over the existence of big dogs. Everyone is obligated to howl in the voice the Lord God has given him."[1] Still, I cannot help thinking that little dogs should keep their howling to themselves.

I talk myself out of my elitism. So many people write memoirs these days, without the slightest compulsion to compare themselves to Tolstoy, and even less to find themselves wanting. We live in a democratic age for a reason. But my doubts do not completely disappear, emerging this time from a different angle. If everyone right and left is writing memoirs, it is the task of the intellectual to ask why now, why memoirs, why everyone, why right, why left. Instead of analyzing the conditions leading to the genre's proliferation, what do I do? I go native, writing a memoir myself. It is no use recognizing that every memoir captures, willy-nilly, a historical moment, unavailable in the same way without it. It is no use recognizing that even the most abstract academic questions grow, not on academic trees, but in the soil of personal life. Some inexplicable unease

---

1    Kirin Narayan, *Alive in the Writing: Creating Ethnography in the Company of Chekhov* (Chicago: Chicago University Press, 2012), 86.

about writing a memoir remains. Since this unease stems from my training as an academic, perhaps that very training can help me get to the bottom of this. What, if any, is the line between humanistic academic analysis and literature? It turns out that even ruminating about this line may require crossing it into literature. Analysis has its limits.

## Voice

At first, it might seem that speaking in a distinctive voice marks the difference between a memoir and more scholarly writing. Yet voice is a very important, even indispensable component in humanistic scholarship. In academic writing about literature, history, art, religion the person speaking is not interchangeable with anyone else, revealing a point of view and a sensibility without which the subject matter would lose one of its dimensions. The goal of those writings, however, remains understanding not the author but the object of study. When I wrote academically about Jewish Communists, for example, no matter how much the point of view remained my own, my voice was never the subject matter itself. In the memoir, my voice is indeed the subject matter, intentionally drawing attention to itself.

Why would anyone want to do that? In the story I tell, much snuffing out of particular voices occurs, whether it be through Communist ideology, through mass deportations to death camps, through my mother's takeover by hostile voices, or through the more ordinary violence of family relationships. I see this erasure of the specificity of persons as an ever-present danger. The authorial voice, basking in its its singularity, counters the theme of erasure. Of course, I did not start out with this strategy in mind. My voice arose without a pre-established plan, and, no doubt, has contributed to my unease about writing a memoir—for to infuse the discreet and often missing "I" of scholarship with a peculiar personality feels like exhibitionism. But then why not write on the subject of the disappeared self in an academic mode, hidden beneath the veil of an impersonal I, which I have also done? I cannot discount the possibility of late-onset laziness. It is difficult hauling around words like "interiority" and "transcendence" over a lifetime of inquiry, especially if the point is not only to clarify their meanings abstractly but to show them at work in the ordinary lives of people. Why don't I tell you about my childhood instead?

But laziness, despite its ring of honesty, may in fact be an inadequate explanation. The departure from an academic mode also comes from a sense of futility. The language that surrounds us, even more so, the objects we live with—the computer screens on devices in cars, homes, offices, street corners—don't make much room for words such as "transcendence" and "interiority," words that imply an unreachable height and depth, not flat surfaces with circuits. We, and this most certainly includes academic theorists about the human, increasingly see ourselves as sets of discrete parts interacting in causal ways with each other and with the environment. We celebrate the formulas that claim to get closer to explaining our behavior and our thinking, more than that, that claim to reproduce them. The battle to escape these formulas is not won by throwing the word "transcendence" around. The best option may be to testify, emphasizing one's particular commitments before a court whose time is not the present. I suspect that most memoirs, even if addressed to contemporary readers, not so secretly aim to reach beyond them. There I go again. The idea of transcendence has made another appearance.

## Poets and Poètes Manqués: Two Movies

If the centrality of voice is one of the marks of literary writing, distinguishing it at least in aspiration from academic writing, this does not mean that literature and humanistic scholarship are completely divorced from each other. Kees, my teacher, was wont to say, with a nod in the direction of E. M. Cioran, that historians of religions are poètes manqués, wannabe poets, failed poets.[2] I have always taken this less than flattering description as a compliment. At least we aimed to emulate the density of poetry, its way of capturing what could not be said in a linear way, even if our expression inevitably fell short of the mark. Scenes from two movies I have seen recently illustrate the density, that is, the poetry, that I am talking about, even if the visual element so crucial for expressing the poetry cannot be shown in the telling.

Much of the Russian film *Beanpole*, set in Leningrad in the immediate aftermath of the Second World War, takes place in a hospital.[3] Among the many wounded and maimed, we encounter a young soldier whose war injuries have

---

2 I am not sure which of Cioran's writings Kees was referring to. The following echoes the same sentiment but about philosophers: "I imagine a thinker exclaiming in a prideful moment: 'I would like a poet to make my thoughts his goal.' But for his aspiration to be legitimate, he would himself have had to spend a long time with poets. . . . Most of all, he would have to know the regret of not being a poet." Émile M. Cioran, *Précis de décomposition: Le Parasite des poètes*, in *Oeuvres* (Paris: Gallimard, 2011), 97. My translation.

3 Kantemir Balagov, dir., *Dylda* [Beanpole], (2019; Russia, Non-Stop Production). The movie is inspired by Svetlana Alexievich's *The Unwomanly Face of War: An Oral*

paralyzed him from the neck down. He banters with his favorite nurse, hiding his pain. His wife comes to visit, probably the first time they have seen each other since the war's beginning. Soon afterward, they plead with the doctor to help him end his life. At first, the latter refuses, advising the wife to help her husband herself through the usual method, suffocating him with a pillow. Something each says makes the doctor relent. He asks the favorite nurse to administer the lethal drug. She balks at doing this again, but finally she too is persuaded. The two scenes that follow have stayed with me in all their thickness, in all that is left unsaid.

In the first, the husband and wife say goodbye to each other at his bedside. She sings a song to him. "You never could sing," he teases her. The only thing she says in return is "Durak," silly man. After a brief silence, he abruptly tells her to leave. They do not embrace; they do not hold hands or say anything more to each other. Outside the hospital, she puts her kerchief back on her head and walks away. That is all. In the following scene, which takes place in the evening, when supposedly everyone is sleeping, the nurse comes in. The soldier assures her that he still wants to go through with it. She administers the drug. They are very close to each other, in the dark. She lights a cigarette, inhales and blows out smoke into his open mouth, lying almost on top of him. He exhales a few times, and then stops. it is a moment of intense intimacy, this accompanying of the dying man in his last moments.

It is as if we were seeing God's back, in the famous passage of the book of Exodus.[4] Moses had asked God to show his glory. God complies, but covers Moses's eyes so that in the end he only sees God's back. It is impossible to see God in any other way, he tells Moses. In the encounters between the soldier and his wife described above, we see the bonds of marriage, the village life from which the song stems, to which the wife will return without her husband; we see their little daughters and what their life might be, and so much else. We cannot say anything about these matters other than that we fail to catch them, although we know they passed by us. In that same biblical passage, God, as he passes, tells Moses that he is a compassionate God. This, in fact, is the central, fleeting presence in these scenes: the compassion of the filmmaker for the husband and wife, the compassion of the husband and wife toward each other—they could not afford to be sentimental—the compassion of the doctor toward

*History of Women in World War II*, trans. Richard Pevear and Larissa Volokhonsky (New York: Random House, 2017).

4   Exodus 33:17–34:7.

the young couple, and the compassion of the nurse toward her patient. Evoking the bleakness of the Leningrad of 1945, the filmmaker also recreates this fleeting but very real compassion. It does not make the circumstances less harsh, less horrific. It humanizes them when it occurs, which is not always. What does it mean that it humanizes them? Maybe that the bonds between people remain, despite the destruction.

The two scenes, through the arrangement of their details, render visible something that nonetheless remains hidden. It requires the heart of the beholder to come to light. After all, the husband is abrupt; the wife's donning of her scarf signals that life goes on; the doctor and the nurse agree to what the law and morality consider murder; the nurse, in lying so close to the soldier, is merely verifying the efficacy of the treatment. Maybe nothing passed at all, or the very opposite of compassion. Compassion is not a matter of rhetoric or prescribed gestures. It lies buried in action, requiring an eye that can find it. The poetry of *Beanpole* lies in evoking through a visual language something that eludes the physical eye alone.

The second film *It Must Be Heaven*, also contemporary, is very different in every imaginable way from the Russian film, except in that it too is poetry[5] Not only is much condensed in each scene but also, unlike *Beanpole*, scene follows upon scene without the glue of plot. They are linked as images in a poem might be linked. The filmmaker, who also plays the chief protagonist, first takes us to Nazareth, to the home of a middle-aged Palestinian man, the protagonist in question. As he sits on his balcony, he notices a younger neighbor, also Palestinian, brazenly stealing the harvest from the trees planted in the grove outside his home. The younger man, once he notices the older man on the balcony, launches into an embarrassed justification. The next day, unfazed, he repeats the same plucking, observed from the balcony as before. In the rest of the movie, much of it taking place in Paris and New York, the middle-aged Palestinian observes events with no apparent connection to the encounter in Nazareth. In a Paris scene, for example, sitting in a cafe, he notices a parade of men and women, all snazzy dressers, walking as if ordinary life meant being on constant, nonchalant display. Beyond the same round, bespectacled face of the protagonist who takes it all in, it would be difficult to point to anything in common with the orchard theft.

---

5   Elia Suleiman, dir., *It Must Be Heaven* (2019; France, Canada, Palestine, Turkey: Rectangle Productions, Pallas Film, Nazira Film, Possibles Media, Zeynofilm).

That face is precisely the common theme. The filmmaker insists on placing that round-faced man in every landscape, taking in the street scene, looking out of the window of his apartment, appraising what he sees, even if we are not privy to his judgment. He remains mute throughout, pronouncing only one sentence in the course of the entire movie: "I am a Palestinian." The muteness may signal his powerlessness. He is, after all, incapable of changing the situations he presents. He retains one power, however, the power to choose which event is significant and simultaneously to expose it to moral judgment. Refusing to leave the scene, the round-faced man introduces a question mark into what we might have come to take as the way things are. Do they really need to be this way? His is a very quiet protest, drawing attention to a judgment that the powerful of this world ignore but that nonetheless operates outside their sphere of influence.

A great deal of humor permeates the film. The scene of the theft of the fruit is a case in point. The tone of the young man is so jovial, so neighborly, as he plucks away. The angles from which the older man's face appears, half swallowed by the balcony wall, no matter how much he attempts to show himself in full, direct some of the humor at him. We are made to understand that the theft and the indignation about the theft are a routine encounter between these neighbors, a ritual of daily life. Similarly, the police hunts that punctuate some of the scenes in Paris and New York have something of the animated cartoon about them, motorized scooters, and choreographed movements, but in the wrong direction. Humor points to the oddity that this is the way it is. It throws into relief the order of the world, creating a non-coincidence with it, if only for a moment.

These movies, each in their own way, raise religious issues without even trying. Compassion and an unassimilable interiority are central vehicles for transcendence in many traditions. To point this out is to mark me as a historian of religions from a certain era. But that is for another essay. Here, all I want to say is that we historians of religions, regardless of our training, are not well equipped to capture the density and humor that these two movies so effortlessly convey. We work with arguments, defend or oppose a theory, lay out evidence in a consequent and logical fashion. All of that is true, and necessary. It is also true, however, that our documents often if not always express not arguments or theses, but thick scenes of human encounter. Much of the world's great religious writing is literature. Much of the history we glean from primary or archival sources breathes with the density of human encounter. And humor, of a certain sort, is often present. At least some scholars are moved by that density, by that humor, and want to emulate it in their own writing. I have to confess that I am among them, desiring to communicate multiple interconnected strands, to hint at incongruity or irony, and to think of nonlinear juxtaposition and humor as an argument against some flat-footed theory or another about the subject. In other words, I have always aspired to be a member of a very particular academic subcategory, that of the poètes manqués. It is not very seemly to be paying oneself what one considers to be a compliment, I know. I wish I could be more modest in this regard, but I am not.

## The Poète Manqué: Jewish Universalism

In a memoir aspiring to the honorable craft of the poète manqué, the more abstract academic questions are never far behind. A poète manqué is, after all, not a poet. It does mean, however, that stories aim to be as important as the abstractions that accompany them, perhaps more important. Take the frequent allusions to the Jewish universalism of my childhood and beyond. Yes, it had an ideological component, and I spell it out here and there. But it was also an atmosphere one breathed, the way people moved their hands and their bodies, their intonations, their facial expressions. I recently saw a documentary about Ethel and Julius Rosenberg, made by their granddaughter, Ivy Meeropol.[6] A good half century after her grandparents' execution, she was lucky to be able to interview a number of their friends, all former Jewish Communists. So many years later, the marks of their ethical passions were still upon them, even if they had not remained Communist, and were now old and bent. It was not so much what they said in response to the granddaughter's questions but *how* they said it. It would take howling with a big dog voice to reproduce the pitch of the voices, the accents, the melodies, the facial expressions through which they expressed their indignation, their protest at the way things are. The biblical prophets surely did not have New York accents and Yiddish intonations. Or maybe they did?

But even a little dog can point out that to be a Jewish universalist in the time and place I am describing, the first half of the twentieth century, maybe a decade or two beyond that, was partially a matter of whom one married, where one was buried, the books one read, what paintings one hung on the wall, if one had them. For the Jewish universalists I knew, it meant Yiddish theater, and it meant fighting in Spain. It meant building the New Man, the physically strong

---

6   Ivy Meeropol, dir., *Heir to an Execution* (2003; USA; HBO).

Jew, but with a trace of humor. My father, as if imitating Romain Gary, although Romain Gary wrote *Promise at Dawn* almost twenty-five years later, reports in 1937 as a soldier in Spain on the battle of Guadalajara to a Yiddish daily in Paris.[7] Having captured three Italian soldiers, he suddenly became afraid, he writes, not knowing what to do next, since he and the prisoners have no language in common. To his relief, they ended up communicating through hand gestures. The scene has the potential of turning into a comic skit, worthy of the Yiddish theater in which he acted. Deflecting the heroic ethic while one is risking one's life has nothing do to with Communism. It does have much to do with being a universalist in a Jewish way.

I tried also to focus on what appear to me to be humorous incongruities. My father's close friends were all Jewish. In my mother's stories about them, two had surnames—Alek Szurek and Oskar Fessler—and three, the closest, did not—Nahum, Edgar, Boris. Some belonged to the party, some did not. All adhered to some form of socialism. Yet, as Jewish as my father's intimate circle was, its members lived with the understanding that to be Jewish obligated one to overlook this detail. The result was, as Jaff Schatz puts it in his book on Polish Jewish Communists, the subset of Jewish universalists I am most familiar with, that Poles could be Poles and Communists, that Ukrainians could be Ukrainians and Communists, but that only Jews could be nothing but Communists.[8] Their fierce universalism made them particular despite themselves. The Jewish social space from which they proclaimed the erasure of the line between Jews and Gentiles brings to mind the "Aleinu" prayer in the daily Jewish liturgy, which concludes every service. In the first stanza, the Jews bow as they thank God for having chosen them out of all the nations of the earth. In the second stanza, they pray for the oneness of mankind. At the end of time, "on that day," all nations, according to the words of the prayer, will bow to the one God as one people. In the old rabbinic notion to which the "Aleinu" gives expression, Jews symbolize today all of humanity as it will become tomorrow. Jewish universalists followed this idea to a tee, except that they skipped the first stanza.

In a less humorous vein, if one chooses to view this as humorous, I want to come back to the fierceness of the ethical passions I mentioned in regard to the companions of Ethel and Julius Rosenberg. It brought back memories of

---

7   *Naye prese*, April 10, 1937, in Diamant, *Combattants juifs*, 109.

8   Jaff Schatz, *The Generation: The Rise and Fall of the Jewish Communists of Poland* (Berkeley: University of California Press, 1991), 142.

Anna Brudny, one of the Jewish Communists I met when I investigated Yiddish theater. Her daughter reported to me, with some impatience, that some years earlier Anna could not be dissuaded from traveling to the Soviet Union to commemorate some important anniversary of the founding of *Sovietish heymland*, the only Yiddish periodical allowed to appear in that country after 1948. From 1948-1952, Soviet authorities had tortured and murdered the main representatives of Yiddish culture. Simply shutting down Jewish institutions had not been enough. How could her mother travel to the Soviet Union to commemorate this token journal, allowed to appear only a decade after the murders, as if this lone publication compensated for the brutal assault on Yiddish culture and Yiddish writers, not to mention all the other horrors? Even if her trip occurred nearly fifty years after the murders, was she not whitewashing Communism in the Soviet Union and elsewhere?

From my conversations with Anna, I know that she had no illusions about the Soviet Union, and maybe not even about the French Communist Party. Yet she would not abandon the tatters of her youthful ideal—the brotherhood of all mankind, expressed in Yiddish. The fact that *Sovietish heymland* was to a degree a Soviet propaganda tool was secondary for her. Primary in her mind was that Yiddish culture was surviving in the Soviet Union, however tenuously. She acted the same way toward *Naye prese*, the Paris Yiddish Communist daily, to which she attended to the bitter end. On some days, I side with Anna's daughter. This is a ridiculous loyalty to a caricature of what Jewish universalism was supposed to be. On other days, I see Anna as she saw herself—unwilling to give up on what was pure in the movement of the heart she experiences as a youth, despite all that went wrong. Read this way, in traveling to the Soviet Union, she was not acquiescing to all the horrors but affirming what all the horrors had obscured. It is customary, when one gets older, to look at one's younger self ironically, and for good reason. But a feature I have found in more than one of my Jewish universalists, whether Bundist or Communist or yet something else, is the unwillingness to sully the ethical command that drove them. How to separate that from stubbornness? I am not sure it is possible. The Jews, after all, are a stiff-necked people.

These contradictions, incongruities and passions are not only those of the generation of my parents. I have inherited them. Despite my great sympathy for the Jewish universalism I came to know, it remains an ambiguous legacy, not only for the murderous side of Communism but also for its homogenizing tendencies. My father and mother spoke Jewish languages, had had some Jewish education, were raised in a Jewish community. I did not. This has led me on a lifelong search to recover what was lost, hoping to discover in Jewish sources and practices a protection against the bulldozing of my own time. I have inherited holes as well as fullness. Perhaps everybody does. Mine is a Jewish story, holes and all.

I submit that literature and academic writing in the humanities meet precisely in the choice to convey the holes, the incongruities, and the passions, in this case, of Jews professing universal brotherhood. The ideas and the holes in the ideas expressed themselves in their apartments, in their cemeteries, and in their marriages, *alongside* their political or ideological activities. The writer of literature and the academic humanist part company only if the latter is determined to pursue the straight line of the railroad track, in this case, the ideologies, rather than the fluctuations on the coast, the life lived, to cite Charles Péguy's comparison between the historian and the memorialist, mentioned in the introduction.[9] They also part company if one is not allowed to cite Péguy because he is not a contemporary theorist. But otherwise a peaceful harmony prevails.

Yet the poète manqué has gotten lost in this description of the meeting point between literary and academic aims. To be a poète manqué is not only to redefine which documents are relevant to understanding a historical moment. It is to fall short of the mark, pointing to what cannot be caught, seeking to show it passing by. The historian of religions is congenitally predisposed to this failure for, by definition, that to which we have given the term religion is too big to catch. Nonetheless we try to catch it, introducing some conceptual apparatus, as I did in describing the two movies, when I extracted compassion and the way it appears from those dense scenes of the Russian film or when I found an interiority not coinciding with the world in the apparently disconnected scenes of the Palestinian film. Neither the word "compassion" nor the word "interiority" appears anywhere in the movies. In using them, I have abstracted from the density, introduced the possibility of a discussion about the source of compassion, what "interiority" refers to, what it means to be human in this time and place. Behind my use of these words lies a long list of thinkers—Pascal, Kierkegaard, Levinas, to name a few with whom I have spent a long time. I am wedded to this combination of dense description and conceptual probing. Conceptual probing, with some luck and skill, can come close to the heart of things. Nonetheless it cannot take the place of poetry. When it comes to compassion and subjectivity, we understand them first and foremost through images and through sto-

---

9    See pp. x-xi.

ries. The conceptual apparatus comes in a second movement to understand what we already know. Conceptual clarity is an essential and nonnegotiable moment, for it allows a questioning and a universalizing that may not be possible without it. It cannot, however, take the place of the first moment, cannot pretend to start from concepts alone, as if thinking meant a closed circle of abstractions. Even this hierarchy needs to be illustrated through a story.

## The Poète Manqué: Walking and Counting Steps

Recently I ran across an article about our increasing reliance on robots in the care of the very old and the disabled.[10] The author describes the research being done to make the robots more "socially sophisticated." They can now not only remind their owners to take their medicine but also give them encouragement, and purr, if they are cat robots. The author is understandably worried about the ethical implication of these devices since their lonely owners, thirsty for human relationship, become attached to these unfeeling mechanisms. I read this article, surprisingly, with a vague sense of boredom. We hear about nothing but robots these days. At what point would robot companions that offer "consoling words to a dying patient" still have been shocking, an unheard of a violation— five years ago, ten years ago? The only remaining problem is not the existence of such programmed consolation but adjusting our morality to include these electronic helpers. It is now share and share alike, some time for the robot and some time for worrying about the robot. "There should be a place in our lives for the softly whirring helping hand and for the unease that true caregiving demands. For care in never a yes or no equation, solved with a new equation or clickable fix. Only by retaining our doubts and hesitations about robots that provide care can we safeguard the humanity of such work."[11]

I sound disappointed, as if I had lost my opportunity to protest against the companion robot or the consoling robot. It is a little bit like my description, in the very beginning of this memoir, of the way we have taken to counting steps, insinuating that in the good old days, we walked, we were organic beings and not data banks, and now that we have gadgets that measure our success or failure to reach ten thousand a day, it is the fall of civilization. Would I have objected to the thermometer, someone might ask, had it not already been around when I was little? Well, a consoling robot is, I believe, not the

---

10  Maggie Jackson, "Would You Let a Robot Take Care of Your Mom?," *New York Times*, December 14, 2019.
11  Ibid.

same kind of device as a thermometer. But who knows? Maybe I would have objected to the thermometer. One can never plumb the depths of one's oddity. Today, in reading about a huge wolf robot in Japan, emitting sixty different kinds of howls to protect city dwellers from bears, I feel reconciled with the world.[12] That robot must be a descendant of the wolf of Gubbio that St. Francis famously converted. Upon hearing the latter's admonitions, the wolf desisted from eating the denizens of the city, placing his paw in St. Francis's hand as a pledge of his peaceful intentions.

To return to the consoling robot, I am not so much protesting my inability to protest as expressing a peculiar joy. I relish catching what these gadgets might mean for our sense of reality, our sense of self and other. There it goes again, I say to myself. A juicy detail has conveniently presented itself, hinting at the world in which we live. The chief characteristic of that world, as I see it, is not that we interact with robots as if they were human. Only a tiny percentage of the population actively does. It is, rather, that our way of apprehending the human is shifting; it is becoming increasingly difficult to see anything wrong with having robot comforters. It is so plausible that lonely older people get solace where they can. It is so implausible to insist, in a population whose life span is now longer than ever, that there will be enough time and people to provide the needed personal care.

The situation of the consoling robot reminds me of a scene in *It Must Be Heaven*, the Palestinian film. In Paris, the round-faced, bespectacled protagonist encounters a homeless man sleeping on a mat on the street. An ambulance arrives, and two attendants pop out. No, they are not taking the homeless man off the street. They come to provide him with a three-course meal, complete with a choice of coffee or tea, cream or black. Then they ride away, sirens screeching, having promised to return. Something is wrong in this scene. The homeless man remains homeless. He is surrounded by social services that remedy everything except the basic condition for which they have become necessary. I wonder if the robot story in the newspaper is not a bit like that. The old and disabled, like everyone else, crave an intimate presence in their lonely moments. They get a computer program instead. An unprogrammed connection with the depth of another being, which engendered the computer program in the first place, is now taken off the table as a basic need. We accommodate to the new order of things. But why stop at the old and disabled? It will save us all

---

12  Elaine Yu and Hisako Ueno, "Japanese City Uses 'Monster Wolf' to Scare off Wild Bears," *New York Times*, November 15, 2020.

time and heartache to interact with something programmed. We are all so busy, and people are so unreliable. Besides, if we want the robot to be more human-like, we know how to program unreliability into the mix.

How preposterous to claim that this describes our world! Sixty percent of people polled object to the use of robots for the care of children or adults, the author of the article tells us. Yes, it is preposterous to claim that intimacy will disappear. But why is intimacy so central, so irreplaceable? Can we articulate it? And will the sixty percent who oppose the use of helping robots continue to oppose them as their sales increase twenty-five percent by 2022, as the author of the article, relying on various industry statistics, also predicts? It is in tackling these sorts of questions that the poète manqué runs up against the usual obstacle. Go define intimacy. Only a story or a poem will do. It is not the end of what can be said—on the contrary, it may be only the beginning. Nothing can be said, however, unless something living and breathing and too big to catch is there first, and remains present, piercing through the analysis. The contrast between the free flow of walking and the staccato of counting steps is a running thread through this memoir. Not in so many words. This "not in so many words" reveals the historian of religions' nostalgia for the poet.

# Acknowledgments

I did not anticipate writing a memoir when I retired from Franklin & Marshall College in June of 2018. Among other projects, I intended to investigate my father's participation in several key moments of the twentieth-century—the Spanish Civil War, the Nazi slave labor camps, Communist Poland in the early 1950s, and much cultural and political activity in-between. *Self-Portrait, with Parents and Footnotes* is what came out instead. It is much more about my mother, who left no historical traces, than it is about my father. *Azoy iz es*, as they say in Yiddish.

As the postscript to this book "Talking to Myself about Literature" is meant to indicate, a certain unease accompanied the writing of this memoir. In my case, it was partially the result of a long practice of writing in an academic voice, although I am sure that my unease is not limited to academics. Writers of memoirs assume that the lives they describe are of interest to a wider public than one's intimates, that they have some historical significance, that they raise questions that others can recognize as their own, that they provide some pleasure in the reading. It is, at the time of writing, an unproven assumption. I want to thank the editors at Academic Studies Press for showing their trust in this endeavor of mine.

I also want to thank the many friends who encouraged me along the way, each in his or her own inimitable style. Some read versions of the manuscript in the making. Their enthusiasm and criticism made it possible to continue. Others offered suggestions for publishers. Yet others offered material help. Some have done all of the above. I will list them in alphabetical order, without further ado, although in reality each deserves a book of praises: Beth Baron, Lina Bernstein, Sonja Bolle, Almut Bruckstein, Galit Carthy, Catherine Chalier, Tamara Eskenazi, Marion Goad, Billy Glovin, Elena Ayala-Hurtado, Patricia Hurtado, David Kramer, Herb Levine, Marilyn Levy, Alan Mittleman, John Modern, Padmini Mongia, Paul Praudel, Michael Steinlauf, Carmen Tisnado, Sarah White, Kerry Whiteside.

In "Russian Friendships," I spoke of the debts I incurred in regard to my parents' friends, which I can never repay. I am grateful to all my friends for having allowed me to accumulate such unpayable debts yet again.

Above and beyond all the other help he has offered, I want to thank Alan Mittleman, for providing me with such good companionship in the last two years.

# Bibliography

## Books

Aleichem, Sholem. *The Adventures of Menahem-Mendl*. Translated by Tamara Kahana. New York: Putnam, 1969.

Antelme, Robert. *The Human Race*. Translated by Jeffrey Haight and Annie Mahler. Evanston: Marlboro Press, 1998.

Camus, Albert. *La Peste*. Paris: Éditions Gallimard, 1947.

_____. *The Plague*. Translated by Stuart Gilbert. New York: The Modern Library, 1948.

Cioran, Émile, M. "Précis de décomposition. Le Parasite des poètes". In *Oeuvres*. Paris: Éditions Gallimard, 2011.

Diamant, David. *Yidn in Shpanishn Krig, 1936-1939*. Pariz: Yidish Bukh, 1967.

_____. *Combattants juifs dans l'armée républicaine espagnole, 1936-1939*. Paris: Éditions Renouveau, 1979.

Esterhazy, Peter. *Celestial Harmonies*. Translated by Judith Sollosy. New York: Echo Press, 2000.

Gary, Romain. *La Promesse de l'aube*. Paris: Éditions Gallimard, 1960.

_____. *Promise at Dawn*. Translated by John Markham Beach. New York: New Directions, 2017.

Kirschenbaum, Lisa A. *International Communism and the Spanish Civil War: Solidarity and Suspicion*. Cambridge: Cambridge University Press, 2015.

Kofman, Sarah. *Rue Ordener, Rue Labat*. Translated by Ann Smock. Lincoln: University of Nebraska Press, 1996.

Levi, Primo. *Survival in Auschwitz*. Translated by Stuart Woolf. New York: Collier Books, 1961.

Levinas, Emmanuel. *Nine Talmudic Readings by Emmanuel Levinas*. Translated by Annette Aronowicz. Bloomington: Indiana University Press, 2019.

London, Artur. *On Trial*. Translated by Alastair Hamilton. London: Macdonald & Co, 1970.

Narayan, Kirin. *Alive in the Writing: Creating Ethnography in the Company of Chekhov*. Chicago: Chicago University Press, 2012.

Pascal, Blaise. *Pensées*. Translated by A. J. Krailsheimer. London: Penguin Books, 1995.

Péguy, Charles. "À nos amis, à nos abonnés." In *Oeuvres en prose complètes II*, edited by Robert Burac, 1268-1315. Paris: Éditions Gallimard, 1988.

_____. "Clio: Dialogue de l'histoire et de l'âme païenne". In *Oeuvres en prose complètes III*, edited by Robert Burac, 997-1214. Paris: Éditions Gallimard, 1992.

_____. "De la situation faite au parti intellectuel dans le monde moderne". In *Oeuvres en prose complètes II*, edited by Robert Burac, 519-565. Paris: Éditions Gallimard, 1988.

Schatz, Jaff. *The Generation: The Rise and Fall of the Jewish Communists of Poland*. Berkeley: University of California Press, 1991.

Singer, Isaac Bashevis. "A Piece of Advice." In *Collected Stories: Gimpel the Fool to the Letter Writer*, edited by Ilan Stavans, 264-271. New York: Library of America, 2004.

Wuzeck, Ephraim, *Zikhroynes fun a Botvinist*. Warsaw: Yidish Bukh, 1964.

## Scholarly Articles

Arendt, Hannah. "Ideology and Terror: A Novel Form of Government." *The Review of Politics* 15, no. 3 (July 1953): 303-327.

## Popular Articles

Gopnik, Adam. "Brevity, Soul, Wit: The Art of the Aphorism." *The New Yorker*, July 22, 2019.

## Films

Balagov, Kantemir, dir. *Dylda* [Beanpole]. 2019; Russia: Non-Stop Production.

Meeropol, Ivy, dir. *Heir to an Execution*. 2003; USA: HBO.

Suleiman, Elia, dir. *It Must Be Heaven*. 2019. France, Canada, Palestine, Turkey: Rectangle Productions, Pallas Film, Nazira films, Possibles Media, and Zeynofilm.

## Archival Material

Institute of National Memory, Warsaw, Poland, file on Jakub Aronowicz, IPN BU 1547/84; IPN BU 0423/3546; IPN BU 0423/3548.

## Rabbinic Sources

*Babylonian Talmud*. Sotah 10b; Bava Metziah 58b.

Rabbi Moses ben Maimon. *Mishneh Torah*, Hilchot De'ot 5:13.

# Index

CPSIA information can be obtained
at www.ICGtesting.com
Printed in the USA
BVHW040730130821
613887BV00004B/66